Praise for *The Next Economy*

"In this eye-opening and thought-provoking book, Ettenberg shows us how to navigate the rubble of the new economy with our profits, our brands, and our sanity intact."

—David F. D'Alessandro
Chairman and Chief Executive Officer,
John Hancock Financial Services
and bestselling author of *Brand Warfare*

"Elliott Ettenberg's view that the next economy is driven by focus, marketing, and customer orientation makes enormous sense. It also makes for a very useful book in keeping a company out of trouble."

—Jack Trout
Author of *Big Brands Big Trouble*

"Wannamaker said 50% of his advertising budget was wasted but didn't know which half. Ettenberg will show you."

—Chuck Peebler
Managing Director, Plum Capital

"Ettenberg raises the necessary question and offers refreshing fundamental insights."

—Dick Blatt
President, Point of Purchase
Advertising International

"Sparing no sacred cows, Ettenberg calls it like it is—and stakes out forcefully how it ought to be. Put off reading this at your own peril."

—Vincent Pica
Vice-Chairman, Voyant Corporation

"It's controversial. It's troublesome. It will keep you up at night. But you have to read it!"

—Bill Turner
President, Merchandising, Marketing, Logistics.
Sears Canada, Inc.

"Ettenberg's central thesis—that commercial success is increasingly reliant on forging a long-term relationship between brands and customers—is right on the money."

—Diane J. Brisebois
President & CEO,
Retail Council of Canada

"*The Next Economy* provides a stimulus for action and a road map to the future."

—Christina A. Gold
Chairman, President, and CEO
Excel Communications, Inc.

"Consumers have won and are spitting out the old marketing techniques. Elliott Ettenberg plots a bold path to their pocketbooks."

—Jim Cannavino
Senior IBM Vice President Retired

The Next Economy

The Next Economy

Will You Know
Where Your Customers Are?

ELLIOTT ETTENBERG

McGraw-Hill

New York   Chicago   San Francisco   Lisbon   London   Madrid
Mexico City   Milan   New Delhi   San Juan   Seoul
Singapore   Sydney   Toronto

Library of Congress Cataloging-in-Publication Data

Ettenberg, Elliott.
  The next economy: will you know where your customers are? / Elliott Ettenberg.
    p.   cm.
  Includes bibliographical references and index.
  ISBN 0-07-137965-7
  1. Marketing. 2. Consumer behavior. I. Title.

  HF5415.E8175 2002
  658.8—dc21   2001044888

McGraw-Hill

A Division of The McGraw·Hill Companies

Copyright © 2002 by Elliott Ettenberg. All rights reserved. Printed in the United States of America. Except as permitted under the United States Copyright Act of 1976, no part of this publication may be reproduced or distributed in any form or by any means, or stored in a database or retrieval system, without the prior written permission of the publisher.

1 2 3 4 5 6 7 8 9 0   DOC/DOC   0 9 8 7 6 5 4 3 2 1

ISBN 0-07-137965-7

This book was set in Janson by McGraw-Hill Professional's DTP composition unit in Hightstown, N.J.

Printed and bound by R. R. Donnelley & Sons Company.

 This book is printed on recycled, acid-free paper containing a minimum of 50% recycled, de-inked fiber.

McGraw-Hill books are available at special quantity discounts to use as premiums and sales promotions, or for use in corporate training programs. For more information, please write to the Director of Special Sales, Professional Publishing, McGraw-Hill, Two Penn Plaza, New York, NY 10121-2298. Or contact your local bookstore.

Contents

Author's Note

The proofs for this book were being typeset when New York City and Washington, D.C., were struck by terrorists. The resulting loss of life was devastating, and the long-term implications for world peace, security, and freedom are still unfolding.

It's clear, however, that the new feeling of vulnerability shared by millions of Americans in the wake of the attacks is having significant economic effects. The retail marketplace, not only in New York City but around the country, has largely collapsed. Of course, our economy had already been struggling in the months before September 11. The softening of demand most consumer-goods companies had experienced in August and early September had been somewhat masked by the mid-year tax rebate. The tragedy simply escalated the slump into a major withdrawal from the marketplace, one that has left thousands of companies stunned and scrambling for answers.

Of course, consumer confidence will recover—it always has. It may have already done so by the time you read these words. But the current drought serves as a sobering reminder of how vulnerable our economy is to customer withdrawal, and how critical it is for businesses to have realistic strategies for dealing with an unprecedented collapse of demand. The 2001 slowdown will be measured in months. The retreat we anticipate (for reasons outlined in this book) is likely to last for decades. We believe that we still have about five years in which to prepare. We hope that *The Next Economy* will help.

Elliott Ettenberg

Acknowledgments

I have been reading books for the better part of five decades, but I never understood until now why authors bother with acknowledgments. Now I understand that an acknowledgment is not simply a public thank you. It's the author's way of recognizing an individual without whose contribution the book would never have come to be.

As a first-time author, I could fill pages with people who deserve my thanks. My acknowledgments, however, are reserved for the following wonderful individuals who treated this effort as though it were their own.

The first is Denise Marcil. Denise and I go back about five years when I first came running to her with the concept that marketing had died and that the business community was still unaware of its passing. She was the one who introduced me to Karl Weber. And she was the one who insisted I focus the book on a broader issue—the remaking of business priorities in a new reality. She shepherded me through the process and acted as a lightning rod on those very rare occasions when Karl and I were getting a little testy. Without her, this book would not have been.

Karl Weber is the consummate scribe. This craftsmanship is evident on every page as he transformed my beliefs into intelligent prose. His ability to ask the right questions and to force me into intellectual corners resulted in a far better book than had I taken any other route. Because he has done this so often, so successfully, I gained the immeasurable benefit of his expertise as a professional business writer. His ability to manage busy authors who are running hectic businesses and are in the air more often than in New York is truly unique.

Karl wrote the book on patience. Without his perspective, his insight, his craftsmanship, and his persistence, this book would not have been.

Mary Glenn is a senior editor for McGraw-Hill. Mary immediately grasped the implication of a North American business model that was broken because it was based on a consumption premise that was no longer valid.

I remember our lunch at Seven, where she talked at length about the impact of the "Next Economy" on business and its subsequent impact on customer relationships. Mary got it. And in future meetings on titles, graphics, and editing, she consistently forced me to deal with the macro implications of the Next Economy. Without her insight and discipline, this book would not have been.

And finally, I want to acknowledge my wonderful wife, Deborah Elizabeth Sharp-Ettenberg. Not for a terrific 15-year marriage. Nor for our 20-year business relationship, working together in Montreal, Toronto, and New York. Not for her supreme confidence in my ability to get out what was inside. But for her most concrete contribution: the book's title. After 10 weeks of effort, none of the previously acknowledged talented individuals were able to create a meaningful set of words that conveyed the message. Deborah uncovered those words one evening driving to our cottage. Without her, this book would not have been.

Elliott Ettenberg

Introduction

Have you noticed that nothing works any more? I'm exaggerating a little, of course. But if your experience is like mine, you probably find yourself feeling more and more dissatisfied with the level of service and the quality of products you encounter. It's true that new technologies have made possible some kinds of service and products that are unprecedented, and some of these are useful as well as cool. But our dissatisfaction as customers continues to grow.

In part, this is because we take new technologies for granted. The curve from "Wow!" to "I've got that" to "Isn't there something better?" keeps getting shorter and faster. In part, it's because technology has raised our expectations so high that there's a real and growing gap between what we expect and what we get.

But our dissatisfaction is also due to the simple truth that the concepts of ultimate convenience, ease, accuracy, speed, and enjoyment promised by what many called the "New Economy" have never been fulfilled. We find ourselves punching numbers on the phone, unable to find a person to talk to. We can't get our questions answered quickly or correctly. We waste countless minutes waiting for the Internet to come online or for our files to download. At a time when leisure is at a minimum, when we're on call 24/7, and when the old dreams of a 4-day workweek and retirement at age 55 aren't even whispered about any more, technology is causing us to waste much more time and experience much more grief than it should.

This is a frustrating situation. For us as businesspeople, it's also a dangerous one. It's dangerous because two-thirds of the economy is based on consumer purchasing behavior. When consumers feel increasingly frustrated, they're apt to cut back on their spending—a trend we already see happening. In time, the rest of the economy is certain to suffer under the impact of this change.

The much-hyped New Economy has been a major contributor to this problem. People no longer have the kind of relationship with favorite brands and the companies that provide them that they had 10 years ago or even 5 years ago. One reason is that in the fervor of the New Economy, all kinds of products and services that weren't ready for prime time were rushed to market. You've heard the rationales: "Speed to market matters most." "Get it out today, and fix the bugs tomorrow." "Early adopters understand the teething problems of new products." As a result, the implied contract between supplier and consumer has been broken. The umbilical cord between brands and people has been cut. Trust has been diminished

Obviously, this is more than a marketing issue. But it creates huge problems for marketers in particular. The central purpose of this book is to suggest a diagnosis—and some solutions.

The truth is that the New Economy was never the Nirvana it was supposed to be. It was really just a bridge between two much more significant and substantial eras, which I call the "Old Economy" and the "Next Economy." The lifespan of both the Old Economy and the Next Economy will be measured in decades; by contrast, the New Economy lasted only months.

The New Economy triggered an important series of changes in our business processes and attitudes:

- It pushed technology into the forefront of the economy.
- It redefined best practices in business arenas ranging from manufacturing to logistics to finance to human resource management.
- It stimulated significant productivity growth in what had been a stagnant economy.

- It rekindled the concept of citizens owning the American economy. (Nearly one-half of Americans now own stock—a situation comparable with the nineteenth century, when Americans owned land, timber, and farms—in effect owning the economy).
- It demonstrated the potential importance of information as a driver of economic growth.

I compare the New Economy with the California gold rush of 1849. Only a small handful of the hundreds of thousands of people lured west by the promise of gold actually became wealthy as prospectors or miners (mainly, the ones who got there first). In that sense, the gold rush was a bust and a fraud. But, if not for the gold rush, the development of the western half of the American continent would have been delayed by a generation or more. This, in turn, would have delayed the realization of the enormous riches generated by California in industries ranging from agriculture to computers to movies.

In a similar way, although the Internet gold rush of the New Economy failed to live up to its billing, it has prepared the ground on which the solid foundation of the Next Economy can now be built.

As you've probably noticed, almost every aspect of business has been reinvented in the last 10 years. Operations have been changed completely, thanks to computerization, just-in-time supply-chain management, accounting changes, and technological breakthroughs in accounting. Information technology departments have migrated from mainframes to personal computers (PCs) to the Internet. Logistics, manufacturing, and distribution have all changed dramatically. Every business discipline has been reinvented except one—marketing.

Marketing has been allowed to languish, gradually losing its ability to affect customer purchase decisions. It's a serious problem, one that you'd think would have received far more attention and coverage than it has.

Why has the problem generally been overlooked during the years of the New Economy? I think there are several reasons:

- The 1990s witnessed the most powerful craze for consumption in North America since the boom of the 1950s. In that environment, there was little perceived need for great marketing. The motto was, "Get it out fast—someone will buy it."

- In the New Economy, business growth was funded by equity rather than debt. Rather than building a brand and a business over time, owners were eager merely to get into the marketplace first and then sell their stock before the bubble burst. Concern with customer relationships took a back seat.
- Value growth in the New Economy was seen as driven by strategic alliances with such high-tech icons as AOL, Yahoo!, and Oracle. But these alliances had everything to do with market credibility and little to do with long-term customer-building.
- Almost no great brand successes were attributed to breakthrough marketing in the New Economy. Instead, the success of such companies as AOL, Yahoo!, and Amazon was attributed to their being first and having the largest budgets and the toughest constitutions—being able to lose money long enough to become profitable.

I'm writing these words in late 2001. The New Economy bubble has now burst. People in business are ready to look forward again—to begin building the Next Economy on a more secure footing. This book is all about reinventing marketing. To accomplish this, a new definition of marketing and a new toolbox of marketing techniques designed for the realities of a new era are needed. We need new metrics that will measure accurately and increase the productivity of the marketing budget. And we need a new management system that will make marketing people accountable for the success or failure of the brands they guide.

These are sweeping changes. But, in a sense, they are a natural outgrowth from the business history of the past half century. Here's the progression in a nutshell:

- The 1960s was all about manufacturing—getting enough goods into the marketplace to satisfy the burgeoning middle class.
- The 1970s was all about finance—getting enough money into healthy companies to sustain their rapid growth.
- The 1980s was all about distribution and efficiency—getting products through channels as inexpensively as possible.
- The 1990s was all about technology and the productivity gains it can bring.
- The 2000s will be all about marketing—about building long-lasting relationships between brands and customers.

Of all the tools available to keep our economy growing, marketing is the most important, potentially the most powerful—and currently the least effective. And because two-thirds of the economy is based directly on consumer spending (with most of the rest based *indirectly* on consumer spending), both the business-to-consumer (B2C) and business-to-business (B2B) sectors will be in deep trouble unless we revitalize marketing. When the consumer stops buying, all of us will end up sucking wind.

This book will contain a little history, especially in the first couple of chapters. But my interest is not in *what* has happened so much as it is in *why*. I will try to come up with a revelation every couple of pages—usually not by describing a trend you've never heard of but rather by linking it to other changes, opportunities, and challenges in a way you haven't seen before.

So let's begin the process of reinventing marketing. Let's explore how tomorrow's skeptical, well-educated, demanding consumers can be convinced to pay a little more for the great brands we will be building in the Next Economy.

1

The Next Economy

From Old Economy to New Economy to Next Economy

We're in the early years of a new millennium, and we find ourselves in an economic climate that is foreign to most businesses. Although there's much prosperity in the land, customers are not buying the way they have historically. Although we have record productivity and relatively low unemployment, we struggle to reach our quarterly sales and profit numbers. So why is it so hard to make money?

I believe the answer is that we are on the threshold of the "Next Economy"—an economy characterized by a huge withdrawal of customer spending, a polarization of North American demand, an exponential increase in demands for service, and a consequent shift in business priorities from satisfying shareholders to delighting customers.

Fueled by aging baby boomers, quality-of-life concerns, nondifferentiated products and services, and the failure of technology to add value to our lives, the Next Economy is about a customer revolution, a rebellion against the self-serving behavior that characterizes today's corporations.

As I will explain, in the past decade we've already passed through one business cycle—the transition from the "Old Economy" to the

"New Economy." The New Economy is already shockingly defunct. *Long live the Next Economy!*

How can we characterize the changes we've been through and the changes that are coming? Here's one way:

- The Old Economy was based on products and services. Success was measured by share of market. The focus of the typical enterprise was on scale and efficiency.
- The New Economy was based on information. Success was measured by time to market and site visitation. The focus of the typical enterprise was on evolving technology.
- The Next Economy will be knowledge-based. Success will be measured by profits and share of wallet. And the focus will be on effectiveness in reaching, serving, and retaining customers.

Marketing will lead the charge in a battle for customer loyalty unprecedented in history. To the few winners will come profits. To the majority will come a slow, agonizing erosion of earnings as traditional business practices fail to turn the tide of softening demand and increasing price erosion.

Existing corporate structures and measurements of success are incapable of guiding enterprise through the coming changes. To survive and prosper in the Next Economy will require a rethinking of corporate priorities and a renewed focus on marketing.

To understand where we're going, we need to understand where we've been. So let's start with a look back at the late, unlamented New Economy.

BIRTH OF THE NEW ECONOMY

On rare occasions, one can sense in real time the moment when a phenomenon passes the tipping point—a time when you realize that you are part of history in the making. By the end of the first quarter of 2000, the tipping point was reached for Internet commerce, the focal point of what was labeled the New Economy.

For several years, interest and participation in the Internet by consumers, businesses, and nonprofit organizations alike had grown gradually. Knowledge of the Internet spread slowly from hard-core "techies" to average computer users, until businesspeople, students, kids, homemakers, and the elderly all began to log on. Then, as the 1998 Christmas season approached, it was as if a bell had been rung. Amid a frenzy of publicity, thousands of companies launched business-to-consumer (B2C) e-commerce operations. Millions of consumers made their first tentative efforts to shop online. The Internet gold rush was on.

In the months that followed, thousands of startups were launched. Some were lavishly financed by starry-eyed venture capital firms. Others were shoestring operations supported by personal credit card debt and long days and nights of work. And thousands of established businesses, from manufacturers and wholesalers to traditional bricks-and-mortar retailers and catalogue companies, established footholds on the Net, trying desperately to hang onto their market position before it was too late.

During 1999 and 2000, the stock valuations of e-commerce businesses experienced a roller-coaster ride. Hundreds of instant multimillionaires were created, at least on paper. This despite a paucity of real profits even for the largest of the Internet businesses and the fact that when and where profits would come from remained largely guesswork.

Today, most of the air has escaped from this valuation bubble. The Internet shakeout has occurred. The much-vaunted Internet-based New Economy is finished. Its longevity was not measured in decades or years but in months.

Most of the business world remains convinced, despite the chaos we are experiencing as the New Economy melts down, that the economic impact of the Internet on almost every business arena will be huge. I agree. E-commerce is here to stay, and it will play a critically important role in the Next Economy. The problem is simply that very few people currently understand its role and its potential impact on us.

After 30 years in the marketing business, working with dozens of companies in industries from retailing, fast food, apparel, electronics, travel, publishing, telecommunications, and auto dealerships—you name it—I've been alternately fascinated, terrified, and bemused by the upheavals of the last 3 years. Five or 10 years ago, executives from new company clients would start their conversation with me by saying, "We're struggling to market our products. What can we do differently?" And I would begin the process of diagnosing and prescribing a cure.

During the 1998–2000 period, the starting point usually was different. New Economy clients walked into my conference room and declared, "We're struggling to market our products. Tell us how the Internet can save us."

Now, at the end of 2001, clients are saying, "We're struggling to market our products. Where are our customers, and how can we connect with them?" It's a lot better starting point than a single-minded focus on the Internet.

Don't get me wrong. For many of the companies I help, the Internet will continue to play a crucial marketing role. But even the pure-play Internet companies have come to realize that while the Net offers unique capabilities for the development of customer relationships, these cannot be built exclusively on information and technology. Thus, while e-commerce is an important business trend and the single most powerful marketing innovation of the past three decades, the real opportunity and potential of the Internet are still little understood by those in business who have the most to gain from it.

The growth curve that the Internet has enjoyed is a phenomenon of historic proportions. Figure 1-1 says it all. The Internet has reached more people, more quickly than any comparable communications innovation. Sheer numbers mean that no one in business—or in any occupation, from government to education, that involves reaching people—can afford to ignore the Net.

The Internet came rapidly into its own as an avenue of trade. During 1999, total e-commerce amounted to an estimated $150 billion. (E-commerce statistics are notoriously imprzecise. The U.S. government, which compiles many of the most important economic statistics, is still grappling with how to track real online business data, with the result that *all* the numbers we see bandied about are somewhat suspect. The figures I'll use, derived from various research studies, are all at

Figure 1-1   Number of years to reach 50 million users.

Radio	38 years
Television	13 years
Cable	10 years
Internet	5 years

Source: Morgan Stanley Dean Witter report.

least of the right order of magnitude.) Of that $150 billion total, some 80 percent involved business-to-business (B2B) selling rather than the B2C marketing most people think of first—Amazon.com, eBay, Priceline, and other icons of the New Economy. Still, close to $30 billion of B2C sales is no mean feat for a medium that barely existed 6 years ago.

The growth of Internet commerce continues to be rapid. By 2004, worldwide e-commerce (including both B2B and B2C) is expected to reach $6.8 trillion. Furthermore, the recent growth of B2C selling, or "e-tailing," has been impressive. Online shopping tripled during the 1999 holiday season (as compared with 1 year before), after quadrupling in 1998, and it continued its rampant growth during 2000. In the United States alone, consumer e-commerce is expected to reach $45 billion during 2001; by 2005, it is projected to reach $269 billion. If growth continues at rates anything like these, B2C selling truly will be a force to reckon with, despite the meltdown of many of the pure-play dotcoms.

Some perspective is in order, however. According to the National Retail Federation, B2C revenues in 2000 for the first time accounted for 1 percent of all holiday sales. This contrasts not only with vastly larger revenue figures for traditional bricks-and-mortar stores but also with catalog sales, which amounted to about ten times the B2C total. Even the most successful e-tailers will never drive their offline competitors out of business—at least not in my lifetime.

Figure 1-2 offers another corrective to the common hyperbole.

Figure 1-2 Reality check: Shopping behavior reported by consumers, past 3 months.

Discount	92%
Grocery	88%
Drug	80%
Department	69%
Specialty	62%
Clothing	42%
Catalogs	47%
Warehouse clubs	42%
Online	11%
TV shopping	8%

Source: Retail Technology in the Next Century: What's "In Store" for Consumers. Indiana University, KMPG Study, July 21, 1999.

To some degree, the hype surrounding B2C selling, especially during the frenzied 18 months between June 1999 and January 2001, outpaced its practical importance. In part, of course, this is simply because B2C selling is still very new. No new way of doing business has achieved liftoff faster than the Internet. But to expect it to overtake traditional retailing within a few years would be unrealistic. Yet the hype and hucksterism that clustered around the Internet (as they will around any perceived gold rush phenomenon) tended to obscure the genuine problems many—even most—e-tailers were encountering in trying to establish any measurement of success in the online world, let alone profitability.

Even more important, few analyzed the development of B2C selling within a larger business context. Most of those who've written and spoken about B2C selling, as well as most businesspeople involved in the field, have looked on B2C selling as a *technological* issue. This is understandable; the technology of the Internet is remarkably innovative and powerful. Making B2C selling into an effective and profitable way of doing business, however, isn't primarily a technological challenge. Rather, it's an economic, social, and psychological problem—in other words, a *marketing* challenge.

The focus on technology rather than on business realities was reflected in the willingness of many venture capital firms to fund e-tail business concepts created by executives with no experience in marketing to consumers. Strange: No venture capitalist would back (say) a real estate developer who was trying to launch a new car company; why were so many venture capitalists eager to back to the same person in launching a dotcom?

To substantiate what was clearly an overpromise and complete lack of understanding of customers, the technology folks committed a classic marketing mistake. They overestimated consumption. They built measurements of success that had nothing to do with profitability (eyeballs, hits, click-throughs, site time), and as the frenzy hit its stride, they launched all sorts of New Economy mergers, based on the Old Economy wisdom: *If you can't generate the numbers, buy them.*

This millennial hyperbole obscured some fundamental business realities that have come back to bite them. The fading of the hype during the "morning after" e-commerce hangover of 2001 is appropriate. Unfortunately, it has been replaced in some quarters by an almost equally exaggerated opposite reaction: "E-commerce is dead," "The Internet is a profitless wasteland," and so on. Not so. A bit of perspective is in order.

THE SHORT, STRANGE HISTORY OF THE NEW ECONOMY

Remarkably, in its brief history (1994–2000), the New Economy passed through at least two distinct phases.

The Banner Years (1994–1998): Eyeballs and Click-Throughs

The first widely adopted model of Internet business was based on using *banner advertising* as a way of attracting visitors to e-commerce Web sites. (You're familiar with banner advertising from the billboard-like ads you encounter whenever you log on to the Net: "Come visit us at Whatever.com.") A variation was for businesses to pay exorbitant fees to appear on popular portals such as AOL, Netscape, MSN, and Excite. The theory was that by buying banner ads on the most frequently hit Web pages, as well as by establishing hot links between pages representing supposedly compatible interests, you could drive a business.

During the early years of e-commerce, many a business plan was built around this assumption. (The embryonic Amazon.com was launched this way.) Unfortunately, the assumption rarely works.

There are a number of reasons why this is so. For one thing, a banner ad rarely offers enough information to provide an incentive to visit the advertised Web site—let alone to buy something there. For another, Internet users soon learned to tune out their awareness of banner ads, especially since the vast majority of such ads were of little direct relevance to them. (If you're logging onto the Internet to do research for a college paper, to check the latest basketball scores, or to chat with an online buddy, why would you be detoured into reading about an online travel agency or clothing store?)

Most significantly, the enormous growth of the Net quickly produced psychological overload for most users. Hundreds of Web sites, all looking more or less similar, sprang up and began competing for eyeballs and click-throughs. In the resulting war of attrition, only a few could expect to survive. As a result, research shows that even when

Figure 1-3 Why users click on banners.

Seeking information	71.4%
Contest	33.8%
Curiosity	33.1%
Cash award offer	10.5%
Affinity	3.4%
Don't know	12.1%
To purchase	0.0%

Source: Jupiter Research survey, August 1999.

banner ads succeed in attracting attention, it's rarely for commercially viable reasons (Figure 1-3).

The banner advertising approach assumed that millions of people would spend 10 hours a day in front of their computers, as if living in a self-contained Internet world. It was a false assumption that showed little respect for the realities of our economy and the real needs and wishes of consumers.

At the heart of its failure, the technologists never accepted the fact that most people used the Net for information, not for transactions, especially in the early years. This wasn't their only misunderstanding. They designed highly sophisticated Web-centric strategies when their target market was operating on computers with (relatively primitive) 486 processors and 28K modems. The techies refused to grasp the huge security concerns average customers had with online transactions. And they never grasped the difference between a label (i.e., a place) and a brand (i.e., a belief).

In the banner years, the common thinking was that no other media were needed to affect sales, that customers understood the technology and appreciated its worthiness, that the customer was as comfortable buying as they were selling, and that their target customers were their peer groups. None of this proved right.

The Brand Years (1998–2000): Awareness and Stickiness

The growing futility of banner advertising led most B2C companies to seek some kind of alternative. Traditional advertising agencies jumped into the fray. "What you need," they declared, "is a brand name that everyone will recognize—the way everyone has heard of Amazon."

(Since Amazon.com had established a successful beachhead in discount online book retailing and were covered daily by the press, thereby becoming practically the only e-tailer most Americans had heard of, it constituted the example everyone sought to emulate.) "Make customers aware of your brand, and your Web site will become *sticky*—a place people will visit and stay."

And because advertising agencies were accustomed to building brand names through image-oriented ads in traditional media, they recommended the same strategy to their e-commerce clients. (When the only tool you own is a hammer, you start to think that everything looks like a nail.) Hence the flood of dotcom advertising on TV and radio and in newspapers and magazines—all the traditional media, in fact—during Christmas 1999 and into 2000.

The pendulum soon swung the opposite way completely. Using venture capital funds in a manner no debtor would tolerate, B2C business abandoned the failing banner strategy and poured millions into traditional media. Most of us still remember the onslaught of 30- and 60-second TV commercials that everyone in the boardrooms liked but which few in the living rooms understood. How many times in 1999 and 2000 did you turn to your spouse and ask, "What the hell were they selling?"

The results, of course, were dismal. If advertising is supposed to build awareness of and affinity for a brand, much of the money spent on dotcom ads was wasted. Test this yourself: Remember the news stories about the many e-commerce ads featured on the January 2000 Super Bowl broadcast? Do you now recall more than *one* of the sponsors? Did *any* of the ads motivate you to make a single purchase?

If your answer is no, you're not alone—and the problem affected not only the Super Bowl commercials but most dotcom advertising. The dotcom ads helped enrich the ad agencies and TV stations, but not the sponsors themselves (Figure 1-4).

The quality of the advertising itself is partly to blame. Most of the e-commerce advertising we see on TV and in the other traditional media is rudimentary at best. Designed and executed by *branded* agencies—that is, agencies with expertise in packaged-goods marketing, as opposed to agencies that specialize in high-transactional clients—the ads conveyed no sense of urgency and provided no motivation to buy. They often established awareness but failed to provide any reason to visit and shop.

Figure 1-4 E-commerce ad spending in traditional media, 1999.

Charles Schwab	$19 million
B&N.com	$18 million
Amazon	$17 million
Priceline	$11 million
CDNow	$9 million
Beyond	$6 million
Outpost	$5 million
AutobyTel	$4 million

Source: Competitive Media Report, Wall Street Journal, 1999.

The result was that the Brand Years failed to transition from site names or labels into true *brands*—that is, names perceived by consumers as having intrinsic *value*, thereby enhancing the products and services attached to them. Figure 1-5 illustrates this vividly. Notice, in particular, the huge gap between the really great brands like Coca-Cola and the still-weak labels attached to even the best-known Internet companies—despite their large investments in advertising.

There were many reasons why the New Economy's life span lasted a mere 6 years. The overriding issue that the technician czars of the New Economy failed to understand, however, is that technology in and of itself adds little value to customers' lives beyond compressing time. And most of the potential savings of time compression are undermined by the complexity and awkwardness of the technology itself. The interface between B2C companies and consumers is so unfriendly that it generates more frustration than it does satisfaction. Thus, there is no long-lasting customer benefit, regardless of what's for sale.

The cheerleaders of the New Economy pinned their hopes on the Internet and on information as the new source of value. They forgot some crucial truths, especially these two: The Internet is just another medium, and information in itself does not add value. *Knowledge* adds value. And for knowledge to emerge from the flood of information in which we're all drowning, customers must be able to access and manipulate that information in simple, easy-to-use ways. The New Economy failed because technology complicated rather than simplified our lives, and we eventually refused to pay for it. Thus the New

Figure 1-5 Brands versus labels.

	Rank	Brand Value
Coca-Cola	1	$83.8 billion
Microsoft	2	$56.6 billion
IBM	3	$43.8 billion
AOL	35	$4.3 billion
Yahoo!	53	$1.7 billion
Amazon.com	57	$1.4 billion

Source: Business Week, November 15, 1999.

Economy was stillborn because it could not evolve into the knowledge economy.

The Transition Years (2001–2006): A Time of Confusion

As I write, the full emergence of the Next Economy is still 4 years away. As with all major sociologic changes, it will happen gradually. We won't all wake up on New Year's Day and herald the arrival of a new era. Instead, we'll look back one day to recognize that we are living in a new world and have been for some time.

The New Economy is being redefined as you read this. Its evolution to a demand-driven economy will take some time to accomplish. But the necessary efforts to develop much better, more accurate customer data, to be proactive in building the customer relationship, and to establish acceptable permission-based relationships are all under way. These are the pillars on which we will begin to build the Next Economy.

Unfortunately, every period of significant change carries with it symptoms of confusion. So these next few years will not necessarily inspire confidence or stability in commerce or the stock market. We have to begin to dismantle the old business models that we built around efficiency and technology and use the pieces to reconstruct a business model based on customer knowledge. This may take longer than 4 years, but the impact of the Next Economy will be felt by 2006 as the evolution of demand-side consumption begins to control the priorities of our businesses.

THE NEXT ECONOMY: KNOWLEDGE-BASED COMMERCE

So the latest shift in the history of B2C marketing on the Internet is already under way. As e-commerce emerges from the meltdown of 2000–2001, the concept of what can be successful online in both the B2C and B2B segments is being redefined. Since the marketplace has rejected placing a value on new information and refuses to patronize pay-per-use sites at sustainable revenue levels, the e-commerce marketplace is in the midst of a metamorphosis toward two extremes.

Megabrand Strategy

At one end are the megabrands. They include the Amazons, eBays, and Yahoos of the world who see themselves as providers of a broad array of goods and services to the household. Their objective is to become the preferred supplier for anything and everything purchased by a particular customer or, better still, an entire household. In theory, if you become the site of first choice, your relationship with the customer will supersede whatever specific goods you may be selling. You'll be the concierge for the household, which in turn will become a reliable source of annuity revenues and profits for years or even decades to come. Hence the intense scramble right now to grab market share, even when it appears unprofitable. The long-term value of the household relationship will make up for current, short-term losses—so the theory goes.

The purveyors of the megabrand idea consider it a new business model suited to the New Economy. Contrast it with the traditional concept of a strong business-customer relationship. The Old Economy model required a business to offer expertise concerning products and services. As a business, your profit margin came from your ability to select, recommend, and market the right mix of products for the customer. The new model says that the only thing that matters is the *customer relationship* itself and that once a company builds this relationship, it can readily transfer the equity it represents into other areas. It's the new version of the old department store concept.

In effect, the megabrand e-tailers say, "We're not experts in any area but suppliers of whatever's available. We don't tell you what to buy; you do the research, decide what you want, and we'll supply it conveniently and at a good price." Thus Amazon can effortlessly add music, then videos, then online auctions, then toys, and then still more products to its online mix with no perceived dilution of the value it offers.

Megabranding is an attractive concept, but it carries with it a serious danger. The danger is that price may be the only differentiator. Lowering your price may capture one sale, one transaction, but it doesn't create the involvement on which customer relationships are built. If the only reason you can offer to customers to encourage them to shop with you is lower price, you are opening the door to any competitor who is willing to accept a smaller profit margin—or greater losses—long enough to grab your market share.

Competing on price alone is a trap into which many of the world's traditional retailers have fallen and from which they are still struggling to escape. More and more megabrand e-tailers have found themselves in the very same trap.

Among the symptoms of the growing futility of the megabrand B2C business model are the following:

- The ineffectiveness of most spending on marketing, as illustrated by the millions spent on advertising by companies such as Pets.com, 1800flowers.com, Living.com, and etoys.com—with little in sales results to show for it
- The proliferation of hundreds of similar sites offering parity product
- Deteriorating profit margins (or increasing losses) due to price pressure
- Continued distrust directed toward B2C companies by consumers
- The increasing power of consumer opinion and advice sites such as CNet, Deja.com, Productopia, Epinions, and Brandwise, which steer otherwise indifferent consumers to peer-recommended products and the lowest-price sites

An ominous sign for megabrand e-tailers is the advent of the *bot*, the software shopping tool that consumers can program to hunt down the best deals in any given product category. The bot isn't concerned about real product value, let alone service or the quality of the customer relationship, but only about price. (This is the same problem now plaguing the business-exchange model in the B2B segment of the Internet.) As bots grow in popularity, profit margins will be driven even lower, putting even more pressure on scarce profits in the megabrand sector.

Another ominous trend is the proliferation of consumer service sites such as mySimon.com, which helps people compare prices from thousands of e-tailers' sites, or DealTime.com, which will search the Net for the best deal in any tracked category, or SonicNet.com, which allows consumers to customize their own list of radio stations. Shopping bots and consumer service sites have decimated the profitability of the B2C space and will continue to do so until price is not the sole reason for shopping the sites.

Microbrand Strategy

At the other end of the e-commerce spectrum from the megabrands are the very small microbrand expert sites, like Autotrader.com, Reflect.com, Electricshaver.com, and Stethoscopes44. EKnitting.com will sell you knitting supplies. Mainlygourmet.com carries top-quality hors d'oeuvres and specialty foods. Evineyard.com will teach you how to choose a great wine and, of course, sell it to you. These are expertise sites, where the depth of knowledge of the subject brings people back to the site. They usually attract a very narrow circle of people who share a passion for the site's content and often have chat rooms where people with a common passion can meet and share their experiences.

These small sites, often started by specialty retailers who went online with a very narrow but very deep assortment/expertise strategy, have continued to grow under the radar of most business reporting. Because they are mostly privately held and have narrow targeting objectives, we rarely hear about them. But many are experiencing 30 to 50 percent annual sales growth.

Sites with this kind of relevance can suspend price as the sole discriminator. These are the hidden backbone of the Web, the places where the technology really does work. They are fueled by customers who share a passion for the site's content and by trust built up over the years—trust that comes from expertise, solid advice, excellent content, and realistic pricing.

These sites do more than facilitate transactional relationships. They are turning into virtual communities of people who share common values. The products they sell are only a part of this value relationship.

These shared values seemingly can suspend price as the predominant component of brand value because the experience justifies the premium price. They grow virally.

Those who've followed the history of business can observe a fascinating historical perspective on the price trap e-tailers have fallen into. At one time, traditional retailers used price strategically to build market share and hurt their competition. Ultimately, this caused a shakeout in which only the strong would survive. In general, the result was that some very big stores and some little stores survived—the big ones using economies of scale to charge low prices and the small ones offering unique merchandise and personalized service—while the middle guys suffered.

The same is now happening in the virtual world. The large will survive based on economies of scale. The small will survive based on service and expertise. Both will have to deliver consistently delightful experiences at all points of customer contact. In between, the midsized B2C company has no future.

THE ROLE OF TECHNOLOGY IN THE NEXT ECONOMY

Some people believe that the current problems of e-commerce are mainly technological ones, susceptible to technological solutions. Some experts say, for example, that more secure payment systems are needed to make more consumers comfortable with shopping online. Various companies are at work on new encryption methods that will make the transmission of credit card information over the Net more secure, and this may encourage some reluctant consumers to take the e-commerce plunge. However, it seems doubtful that concerns about security have been a major factor in the depressing growth of B2C marketing. Very few instances of online theft have been reported, and the few well-publicized technological snafus caused either by incompetence or by unscrupulous hackers have victimized businesses rather than individuals—for example, the February 2000 attack that tied up some of the most popular e-commerce sites by flooding them with voluminous queries.

Other technophiles say that the slowness of most current Internet connections is a major source of customer frustration. This will be alleviated, they say, with the arrival of broadband in the home—cable modems or DSL lines rather than the dialup modems now widely used. (AOL's purchase of Time Warner was motivated in part by the desire to get access to Time Warner's home cable systems.) Again, it's possible that this innovation will speed the migration to e-commerce. In itself, however, the need to save time scarcely can be a major deterrent for most consumers, since even at its slowest, online shopping is faster than driving to the local mall for a shopping trip. And most people already feel that they're moving through life as fast as possible: When you're going at full speed 24/7, why would you want to try to make it 25/8?

Still other experts look to the advent of new appliances for accessing the Internet as the Holy Grail of e-commerce. Already some wireless devices are capable of being hooked up to the Web, and new forms of interactive TV, which will allow you to shop from home by pressing a button on your remote to order, are under development. (Again, AOL and Time Warner are positioning themselves to play a leading role—so they hope—in this arena.)

We see the Web as another form of media, one that is information-driven rather than entertainment-based. Unlike the personal computer, TV is a family medium, a point of conversation and a shared social experience. When you watch TV, you're 6 to 9 feet away from the set, not 2 feet away as when you look at a computer monitor. TV is about content—drama, comedy, sports—with commercials inside the content; by and large, the mood is relaxing. By contrast, the computer is about information; the mood is active, tense, involving. It is also transactionally effective. If your megabrand business model is based on the idea of capturing the purchases of an entire household, then moving from the PC to the TV may be a positive step. If you're a microbrand business, then your success in the Next Economy should be tied to a Web-centric strategy. If you are in between, you've got a serious challenge ahead of you.

Regardless of what your strategy is in the Next Economy, technology will not be allowed to repeat the fiasco it precipitated as the catalyst for the demise of the New Economy. The harnessing of technology and management's ability to ensure that it serves the customer and the corporate priorities are among the prerequisites for success in the Next Economy. The purposes of technology in the coming decade will be to simplify, not to complicate. To reduce learning time. To facilitate customer adoption. To personalize the experience. And finally, to enhance the value of the brand.

BABY BOOMERS, TECHNOLOGY, AND THE FAILURE OF THE NEW ECONOMY

We have all heard a lot about the influence and importance of the baby boomers. Some might even say that they've heard too much about them. Perhaps so—but their significance as the largest generational cohort in world history is difficult to overstate.

One proof of the economic significance of the boomers lies in this fact: *The failure of the New Economy can be attributed in large part to its failure to engage the commitment of the baby boomers.*

Think about it. The short-lived, Net-centric, dotcom-oriented New Economy, which was supposed to revolutionize forever the way we all lived, worked, and played, was *not* a baby-boom phenomenon. In generational terms, it was a gen-X product, but more to the point, it was built *by* geeks *for* geeks. This is why it never really took over as advertised. Neither geeks nor gen-Xers have the economic power in our society. The baby boomers do.

One problem with the New Economy was that it turned off the powerful, affluent members of the baby-boom generation. Remember, although the boomers grew up with television, they are not a particularly technophilic group. They are far less tolerant of technology and its flaws than the gen-Xers are. A 22-year-old may consider the fact that his or her computer crashes and his or her Internet service provider (ISP) fails just another technology challenge: "It's a computer; what do you expect?" But a baby boomer expects his or her computer to work just the way his or her telephone always has. Baby boomers were raised never expecting a product to *not* work. Thus, with inevitable exceptions, baby boomers never whole-heartedly embraced the technological promise at the core of the New Economy.

Isolating the baby boomers from the rest hurt the geeks of the New Economy. Half-consciously, they were building technology not for every consumer but for an elite group. The rest of us find the current state of most digital technology exhausting and frustrating. Most of us have cell phones, but they break down, the connections are not very good, service disappears at arbitrary times, and no one understands the bills. Our computers crash, offering cryptic and vaguely insulting messages as "explanations" of the problem. Surfing the Net means wading through 10 irrelevant and annoying Web sites in search of the one that contains information or service of interest to us. And so on. The truth is that most of us—especially baby boomers—have problems dealing with almost every aspect of technology. And this is one reason for the failure of the New Economy. The technology on which it was supposed to be built is not yet user-friendly (with the single possible exception of e-mail).

Nor is its impact on our lives completely benign. Before the advent of the New Economy, futurists talked a lot about the glut of leisure time that "automation" and growing affluence would bring us. There were predictions about 4-day work weeks and the vastly improved quality of life this would bring us. These ideas now seem painfully quaint. Today, everyone seems to be carrying a cell phone and a personal digital assistant everywhere and is checking back with the office constantly. The phrase *24/7* has become depressingly familiar. Vacations are measured in days, not weeks.

The coming of the Next Economy will correct this.

G2G Marketing

The avatars of the New Economy also were guilty of several other crucial misunderstandings. They failed to recognize that women are the mainstays of the economy—the chief financial officers (CFOs) of the household, as I've called them. The world of digital technology was launched with a sharp tilt toward males, and in business terms it largely remains a universe in which young men are talking to other young men rather than communicating with the real buyers of the world, who are overwhelmingly female. I call it geek-to-geek (G2G) marketing. It certainly wasn't getting through to anyone else.

Some of the manifestations of this failure to connect were fairly subtle. For example, there was the widespread belief in the New Economy that intrusive banner ads were an effective way of reaching Internet users with a commercial message—in fact, the more intrusive, the better. Aside from the other problems with this philosophy, one major drawback is that most women I know hate banner ads. Just as they don't enjoy having a salesperson sticking his or her nose in their faces when they're browsing in a favorite store, they don't like constant interruptions when they're surfing online.

In the New Economy, the geeks believed (and claimed) that it's possible for people to have a relationship with technology. Maybe that could be true if the technology were passably reliable—maybe. In reality, however, people have relationships with people, not machines. In the New Economy, there weren't enough people talking to people—and especially women talking to women.

THE E-COMMERCE SHAKEOUT

As I write, the e-commerce shakeout is largely complete. Just five Web sites—Amazon, eBay, AOL, Yahoo!, and Buy.com—dominate B2C sales. Thousands of e-tailers staked their fortunes on the hope of breaking out during the last two holiday seasons; hundreds have shut down as a result of their inability to do so.

What separates the few successful e-commerce companies from the hordes of failures? It's the same thing that separates successes from failures in traditional retailing: *Rather than simply satisfying demand, they delight their customers.*

The Next Economy will prove that e-commerce is not a technology business, a database business, or even a product-based business but a *service* business. The Internet is simply the communications component of this business, not a business in itself.

As a result of this misunderstanding in the B2C segment, even the rudimentary service standards that most traditional retailers strive to meet are violated routinely by e-tailers (Figure 1-6).

The direct consequences are clear. A recent survey indicates that over half of would-be online shoppers—63 percent to be exact—canceled orders after hearing about the outrageous shipping and handling charges. As long as B2C customer surveys show numbers anything like these, the growth of profitable e-commerce will be severely limited, and business failures will continue to mount.

RETAIL VERSUS E-TAIL

The pioneers of e-commerce, even the successful ones, largely ignored issues of customer service—even such basic issues as order

Figure 1-6 Most-cited online customer service issues.

- 63 percent terminated an online transaction because they couldn't find the right information.
- 42 percent had to wait longer than 5 days for a response to an e-mail query.
- 40 percent complained about the lack of live support.
- 36 percent of customers who research a product online buy it offline.
- 26 percent say they were totally dissatisfied with the online shopping experience.
- Visitation/transaction conversion rates = 0.1 to 3.0 percent

Source: Ellen Jovin and Jennifer Lach, "Online with the Operator," *American Demographics Magazine*, February 1999.

fulfillment and shipping. But what often goes ignored is the comparably dismal performance of traditional retailers in the same time period. One might think that customers who abandoned e-commerce would revert to their familiar retail shopping habits. This didn't happen.

We know that the rate of abandonment of e-tail shopping carts is very high—up to 60 percent. But retail abandonment rates are in the 70 to 75 percent range. This means that three-quarters of the people who take the trouble to walk into a store are unable to find anything they want to buy. Is service a problem in e-commerce? Definitely—but it's a huge problem in offline merchandise as well.

The business press has done a good job of documenting the problems with security of customer information (such as credit card numbers) in online selling. The truth is that customers can be cheated equally when the sales associate, waitress, or automobile mechanic walks away with the credit card to process the sale. Similarly, problems related to unsolicited sales pitches and the unauthorized dissemination of customer data are hardly unique to the online world—just survey the piles of junk mail you receive or consider the number of unwanted telemarketing calls you get. The fact is that customers are just as vulnerable—and just as badly abused—offline as they are online.

THE VITAL INGREDIENT IN THE NEXT ECONOMY

In the Next Economy, without a high standard of customer service, no true business-customer relationship can exist. If all you get is a transaction, you'll fail. It's a lesson almost all e-tailers—and not a few traditional retailers—have yet to learn.

In truth, the customer service problems that plague both B2C marketing and retailing are highly solvable, provided that a strategic commitment is made by the business to solving them. Furthermore, the Internet itself can play an important role in enhancing service, to the point where the crucial level of *delighting the customer* is attained.

One of the many ironies of the brief history of e-commerce is that according to its early avatars, the Internet was supposed to effect "disintermediation," the elimination of virtually all intermediaries from business. Now, the most successful e-commerce Web sites themselves have become intermediaries, merely taking products manufactured by other companies and having them shipped out to customers in exchange for a (very small) slice of the action.

In the long run, however, the gurus of disintermediation may prove to be right after all. Most e-tailers, in their role as intermediaries, are doing little to add value to the customer experience. Hence the intense downward price pressure, which is only increasing with every quarter: Customers believe that the only benefits they get from doing business online are convenience and price. In the end, no company can thrive under such circumstances.

The winners will be the companies that figure out how to take the next step in the development of the Internet—using online technology as a way to improve, enhance, personalize, and deepen customer relationships.

More and more e-commerce managers are finally coming to realize this truth: Opening a dotcom business is just like opening a store. If all you do is hang a sign above a storefront, who cares? Shopping habits will not be altered unless something more happens.

Ultimately, every e-tailer—and every traditional offline marketer—must figure out how to build a business based on its relationships with customers. Great technology is not enough—in fact, it's not even the first step in solving the equation. What counts is using the technology to *customize* your offerings to meet the unique interests and wants of individual households and customers. And equally important is offering the opportunity for customers to provide *real-time feedback* about their satisfaction, frustration, desires, and preferences, enabling you to perfect your business in compressed time.

Only by using technology in these ways will you attract customers to visit your business over and over again and buy from you repeatedly, creating a steady stream of revenues and profits that will sustain your organization and make it possible to grow. This type of customization is what the emerging Next Economy will be all about.

THE EVOLVING CUSTOMER RELATIONSHIP

In the Old Economy, the customer relationship was based on maximizing transactional profit. Over time, shopping aisles got smaller, special sales got closer together, service was cut back, and merchandise was increasingly cost-reduced, until customers pushed back by switching brands or stores. The customer relationship could best be described as *abusive*.

In the New Economy, the relationship between the customer and the Web site was decidedly one-way. Banners intruded on customers' browsing. Cookies were left behind to trace Web browsers' travels (unbeknownst to the browsers), and the resulting information was then used to manipulate their behavior or sold to other e-tailers. The relationship could best be described as *victimizing*.

The growth in customer knowledge and power promises to overturn these old and unfair models of the customer relationship. In the Next Economy, the relationship will be based on customer service. And it will be described as *responsive*.

The key to the Next Economy lies in developing new tools for building brands—tools adapted to the new marketing environment we find ourselves in at the start of the new millennium. The old methods just don't work any longer. But a new set of tools, core competencies for the coming decade, holds the promise of creating a new contract with the customer—one that is as meaningful to tomorrow's consumers as the old contract was to their mothers. And although the Internet is not a cure-all for the impotence of today's marketers, it can play an enormously positive role when used to implement the right set of marketing tools.

The new tools marketers must learn to master include

- *Want segmentation.* In the postwar world of the 1950s, 1960s, and 1970s, when most customer spending was driven by *needs*, the challenge for most businesses was simply to keep up with customer demand for more and better products. No more. Customer spending today is driven by *wants*. To understand these, marketers must learn to segment and target customers in terms of their values, associations, and loyalties.
- *Quintile management.* Not all customers are created equal. In the Next Economy, your objective must be to target *fewer* but *better* customers. As increased sales become increasingly elusive, increased *profits* are still attainable—by reaching the right customers. A marketer who identifies and understands best customers can then develop marketing strategies that will maximize the "share of wallet" the company receives from them.
- *The four R's.* This is a new marketing toolbox designed to replace the four P's on which generations of traditional marketers have relied. The four R's—Relationships, Retrenchment, Relevancy, Rewards—represent four basic marketing strategies, each with two associated core competencies, around which today's most successful businesses are already being built.
- *Comarketing.* Many companies already use forms of *vertical comarketing*, in which (for example) retailers and manufacturers team up to share advertising and promotional costs. In the near future, *horizontal comarketing* will explode in importance as retailers, manufacturers, and service companies increasingly organize their efforts not around products but around categories of customers with parallel wants.
- *Delighting customers.* Although the words *consumers* and *customers* are often used as if they are interchangeable, they're really not. Consumer-driven marketers are concerned mainly about the quantity of sales they can generate; customer-driven marketers are concerned mainly about the quality of the relationships they can sustain. The most successful marketers of tomorrow will do more than sell to consumers; they will delight customers and so develop long-term, continuously reinforcing, highly profitable relationships.

This combination of new tools can enable most businesses to successfully leapfrog the transition to the Next Economy. Unfortunately, the time to act is short. The cumulative social and economic forces that have produced the dilemmas today's marketers face are continuing to gather strength; they'll crest in the early years of the coming century. To fully grasp the nature of the Next Economy and the significant steps we have to take to flourish in it, you need to understand its larger causes. I will address this topic in the pages that follow, before offering my detailed prescription as to what marketers must do—whether they transact business online, offline, or both—to survive and thrive in the years to come.

Marketing Impotence

Scan back a single lifetime and consider the social and economic changes our world has experienced: the trauma of a Great Depression, a global war more terrible than any in history, and the emergence of a new Europe, a new Japan, and scores of developing nations; the birth of one new industry after another, from TV and home electronics to computers and biotechnology; the development of mass movements on behalf of the rights of minorities, women, and homosexuals; the sudden collapse of the Soviet Union and the end of the Cold War; and the information and Internet revolutions in industry, education, entertainment, and government. Most recently, there's the terrorism of September 11, 2001. It amounts to enough change for several lifetimes.

I have lived through my share of these troubling, exhilarating, amazing times. I have helped many businesses navigate the ever-shifting economic currents these multiple changes have generated. Thirty years in the marketing business, working with clients in a host of industries, from packaged goods and pharmaceuticals to cars, cable TV, and retailing, has provided me with some perspective on change and how to survive it. Most "revolutions" turn out to be more like noreasters than tidal waves: stormy, noisy, perhaps risky for the unprepared, but sure to blow over in time, leaving the landscape pretty much as it was beforehand.

Thus it comes as a bit of a shock to me that I find myself saying, as I look around the business world at the start of a new millennium, that I am frankly scared. The more I study the signs around me, the more I see the coming decade bringing a series of social and economic changes that will cause a business upheaval unlike any we have seen in generations.

What's more, this upheaval is really not a matter of theory or speculation. It's the inevitable result of trends in technology, demographics, society, and the economy that are already well advanced—trends that are no longer possible to reverse or alter, if they ever were.

What worries me is not just the upheaval that I see approaching. I think the changes we face are well within our power to survive. My fear is that so few people are anticipating what's coming. If we in business fail to adjust in time, the results could be devastating: the collapse of thousands of businesses, the loss of millions of jobs, the destruction of billions of dollars in wealth.

The underlying characteristic of the Next Economy is a huge change in consumer demand caused by baby boomer demographics. Older households simply buy less, and baby boomers, like all of us, are getting older by the minute. One American turns 50 every 6 seconds. As this begins to have an impact on the economy, the inevitable slowdown in demand will affect us all.

Aggravating this softening in demand will be the split between have and have-not households. Most North American businesses that cater to the customer are centered under the bell curve. They market goods and services to the middle class of America, where most of the volume is done. In the Next Economy, businesses will have to cater to one extreme or the other. The middle will be unprofitable. This is a reality that affects over half the consumer goods and services businesses operating today.

For those whose livelihood depends on consumer purchasing, the coming upheaval will hit especially hard. Estimates vary, but by most accounts, fully one-third of all workers are involved in marketing in one way or another: some 20 percent in retailing alone and the rest in promotion, public relations, advertising, or selling or distributing goods. And of course, every business ultimately depends on marketing, in the largest sense of the word: Nothing happens in any industry until a customer's wants are met, a product or service is delivered, and a sale is made. Thus, even if you don't happen to have the word *marketing* in your job title, the chances are very good that you will be affected by the coming changes.

When you consider that two-thirds of all gross domestic product is driven by consumers, there are really very few pure business-to-business (B2B) corporations. Most of these are simply supplying goods and services to other companies who deal directly with customers. Thus any significantly prolonged change in consumer buying behavior affects all of us in business.

Within a decade, the Next Economy will bring to an end virtually all our traditional ways of doing business, particularly the old ways of marketing products and services that have served North American businesses reasonably well for the past 50 years.

If this surprises you, that's understandable. In a number of superficial ways, our economy today still appears robust. Unemployment is low, and so is inflation, still the great bogeyman feared by most businesspeople. On paper, more people have accumulated greater wealth in recent years than ever before: 50 to 60 percent of Americans now participate in the stock market, and after decades of soaring share prices, many are feeling flush, even after the recent stock meltdown. Recent government statistics even indicate that household incomes have begun to creep upward after years of stagnation. The Federal Reserve (Fed) is doing a fine job. At a glance, the economic news appears far from disastrous.

However, even as we enjoy the pleasant sunset of an era of remarkable growth, danger signs are accumulating. The average family's liquidity—the amount of emergency cash people can get their hands on if they need it—has fallen to below 90 days' income. Thus the typical North American family is one bad quarter away from losing the paper wealth they enjoy. The savings rate, which has been shrinking for decades, is now negative, while household debt is at record highs; people are spending money as fast as they make it, or faster. And most households now rely on two wage earners, not one, with more and more workers moonlighting at second jobs or taking on all the overtime they can handle. Are we doing all right financially? Yes, at the moment—but only because we're running as fast as we can.

Families today are so badly stretched for money, time, and other resources that significant changes in consumption will affect the economy dramatically. Things right now are as good as they're going to get. Business can cost-reduce itself down to just-in-time (JIT) inventory, production, and people, increasing productivity significantly, but leaving itself no room for margin should demand soften significantly. Downsizing at warp speed is a new mission-critical capability for North American businesses—a capability aptly demonstrated during the tech meltdown of 2000–2001.

Business is so precarious that a handful of changes can easily bring the whole house of cards down around us. Some of these changes are already under way: greater security, higher inventories. And many of the early warning signs are visible in the marketing arena, where shifts in consumer demand are felt first.

Although the details of the Next Economy debacle will be news to many businesspeople, the notion that marketing is in deep trouble will not be. The truth is, anyone who's been paying close attention realizes—or at least suspects—that marketing has already lost its effectiveness. In fact, I describe the current state of marketing in North America as *impotent*—a word that might seem funny if I didn't find so many businesspeople shaking their heads in rueful agreement when I use it.

Marketing impotence is an affliction that is slowly draining the lifeblood—profits—out of thousands of businesses in every industry. It's an all-too-predictable consequence of our failure to recognize or understand the changes happening under our feet—changes that portend the major social and economic upheaval currently taking shape just over the horizon. Marketing's inability to do the very thing it is responsible for—building brand value with its customers—has been evident for a long time. The difference between the Old Economy, the New Economy, and the Next Economy is that in the former two, exponential growth masked the declining ability of marketing to build relationships with its customer base.

In the Next Economy, growth is not a given. Retrenchment and softening of demand are characteristics of what's ahead. The vulnerability of corporate marketing will be exposed quickly once a contracted, deflationary marketplace begins to be felt.

Here are some of the symptoms of marketing impotence. I've heard them described, in varying language, by executives from scores of businesses. They form a pattern of interrelated problems, all pointing to the same underlying cause. How many do you recognize from your own company?

THE SYMPTOMS OF MARKETING IMPOTENCE

Shrinking Customer Loyalty

The mantra of every business, of course, is *growth*. Each of us in business, from the chief executive officer (CEO) to the sales associate, is measured by our ability to deliver annual increases in sales and profits. Stop growing, and you create opportunities for competitors, in other companies and even other industries, to steal your customers, slowly or quickly draining your company's lifeblood. You find yourself back on your heels, in defensive mode—and in business, as in war, you can't win battles when you've circled the wagons. It's not a question of whether you'll get overrun—just a question of when.

In the decades since World War II, marketers in North America have become accustomed to enjoying robust growth. From the 1950s to the 1970s, huge social, economic, and demographic forces were working on our behalf. The baby-boom generation—history's largest cohort of consumers—was growing from childhood into adulthood, and their buying power was increasing with each life milestone they passed. The economy was flourishing, thanks to a host of factors from new technologies to the steady stimulus of Cold War defense spending. A powerful new medium for communication and advertising—television—enthralled Americans and helped weld them into a vast mass market for whom the great brand names they saw on TV—Coke, Ford, Sears, Zenith, Disney—were almost magical in their allure. Throw in a dose of price inflation, and it was easy for marketers to boast healthy looking sales increases year after year. The biggest challenge for many companies was keeping up with demand. In the postwar world, growth came naturally.

Is this the same world you're doing business in today? You know the answer. If your business is like most others, you're finding it more and more difficult to retain your traditional customers—let alone to grow your sales based on increasing business with them. Customers no longer seem to respond to your brand names the way they once did; they seem shockingly ready to shift their business to your rivals from around the corner or around the globe, even to no-name, private-label brands or to upstart firms that may not have existed 5 years ago. It's not your imagination—and it's not your business alone. In industry after industry, customer loyalty is withering—as are the prospects for easy, "natural" sales growth.

Unable to retain their old customers and grow with them, businesses of every kind are resorting to more and more desperate measures in search of sales increases. Retailers plagued by flat or declining same-store sales find themselves pushing to open new outlets in ever-more-remote regions of the country or the world or trying to squeeze in one more store in towns already saturated with places to shop. Manufacturers find themselves straining to prop up their distribution systems, paying ever-increasing "slotting allowances" or "coop advertising" moneys to retailers in order to induce them to keep their brands in front of customers. These artificial stimulants have become the norm in most businesses; for many retailers, they represent the difference between red ink and black, and for many manufacturers—especially those whose brand names rank fourth or lower in the hierarchy of their industry—they are the last defense against a complete sales collapse.

Reliance on such forms of brand support is a warning sign. If your brands had enough value in themselves, it wouldn't be necessary to pay retailers to support them; instead, customers would insist on having access to them. If you find that you're not only forced to pay retailers to promote your brands but that the amounts you must pay seem to grow every year, it's clear that you and your brands are in serious trouble. The payments you're making are like relying on a pacemaker rather than a healthy heart—they can keep you alive, but they can't reverse the underlying problem of shrinking customer loyalty and withering brand value.

Declining Banner Loyalty

I am always surprised when I work with major retailers and they open their marketing books to me to find that even the best retailers don't enjoy much banner loyalty from their customer base. In most cases, I have found that customers short-list-shop banners just as they do brands. As a result, most retailers supply less than half their customers' demand in their category. And this means that they share each customer with at least two other retailers and that the customer views this retail relationship as anything but monogamous.

Thus, if you're a grocer, you're almost certainly selling less than half the food eaten by your most loyal customers. A generation ago, this wasn't true; the typical family had a favorite food store at which they stocked up on everything from the fixings for Sunday dinner to their favorite snack foods. If a certain brand of cereal or frozen vegetable wasn't sold at your supermarket, you just didn't eat it.

Owning the "food franchise" in a particular town gave a retailer tremendous clout. It also gave the packaged-goods marketers a simple, convenient way of getting their products in the hands of shoppers. Whatever economists might say about the virtues and flaws of oligopolies, there's no doubt that a retail oligopoly, in which a business is dominated by just a few big stores, offers great economies of scale to marketers.

Today, the retail landscape has fragmented. Let's stay with the food business as our example. Most people are eating more meals away from home, whether at fast-food stores, sit-down restaurants, or snack bars at work or play. The big stock-the-shelves shopping trip is becoming a rarity; with more and more dual-income families short on time and energy, people find themselves buying take-out meals, ordering food for home delivery, or stopping off at any convenient store on their way to or from work, school, or the kids' activities. Think Boston Market or Foodini's, a new chain of takeout pasta shops owned by Chevron—that's right, the oil company—and located right in the service stations. When people get hungry today, they no longer automatically turn to their favorite A&P, Safeway, Albertson's, or Public's; instead, they may drop into any store from 7-11 or Sam's Club to McDonald's or Foodini's. No single retailer dominates the food franchise in a particular town any longer.

An analogous change has occurred in almost every retail and product category. Not so long ago, if you wanted to buy a pair of sneakers, you visited the shoe store on Main Street; for the latest music, you visited the local record store; for a dozen breakfast rolls, you visited the bakery. Today, *everybody sells everything*. You can buy sneakers at a convenience store, CDs at a drug store, and rolls at a filling station—or buy all three at a discount club and, while you're there, get a prescription filled, have your car's tires rotated, and withdraw cash from your bank account.

It's no wonder that *retailer infidelity*, once a minor problem, is now the rule rather than the exception. Your customers no longer need to plan a trip to your store to buy what you have to offer. Chances are they can get it anywhere. As a result, it's no longer enough to be "the shoe store," "the hardware store," or "the restaurant" in town. You now need to create a unique and compelling reason why customers should do business with you. Suddenly the marketing challenge is an entirely new one—and a much more difficult one to master.

Consultant Fred Reichheld of Bain and Company has made a specialty of examining the phenomenon of customer loyalty more deeply than anyone else. He estimates that the average U.S. corporation now loses *half* its customers every 5 years. That's the average—many companies are doing worse. We all know how much more difficult and costly it is to find a new customer than to retain an old one. No wonder so many of us in marketing feel that we're scrambling faster than ever just to stay even—we are.

Disarray in the Marketing Department

Losing customers is only one part of the vicious "loyalty drain" cycle. According to Reichheld, the typical American corporation, which loses half its customers every 5 years, also loses half its employees every 4 years and half of its investors *every single year.* These phenomena are closely interrelated. As customers drift away and we in business scramble to replace them, we engage in increasingly desperate strategic and tactical ploys—"reinventing" our brands and our companies, shifting from one target market to another and another, and concocting ill-conceived spin-off products and services that we drop almost as quickly as we introduce them. Sometimes we succeed for a quarter or two; sales and profits respond, at least temporarily, and Wall Street rewards us with a spike in our stock price. However, if we haven't solved the underlying marketing problems, we inevitably hit the wall again in 6 months or a year. The trends curve downward, and the churning starts again.

In this kind of unstable business climate, it's natural that employees and investors churn *their* assets, too, in an unending yet ultimately futile search for a safe haven—a place where they can invest their time, energy, and money for long-term productivity and satisfaction. However, very few businesses today offer such secure long-term prospects.

One result is that talented people in North America today rarely make marketing a lifelong career. When they do, they almost never stay with one product, one brand, or one company for long. Typically, young marketers are given responsibility for a particular brand; they spend a year or two jacking up its short-term sales in any way they can, often through price-based promotions that shred the brand's long-term equity. They are in a pyramid structure where for every five people, there is one job above. They are often being judged on the basis of sales growth or market share. Their individual goal is to use their steward-ships of the brand as a springboard forward in their career.

Those who succeed are then elevated to another level of the organization, leaving the brand in the hands of yet another fledgling marketer. The result is that brands are chronically in the hands of young, inexperienced people with no institutional memory or commitment to long-term growth.

If you help to run a marketing department or have a position in advertising, public relations, or one of the other related fields, you're familiar with this phenomenon, as well as with the inadequate solutions most companies attempt and the chaos they cause through periodic management upheavals. Many organizations, aware that they're lacking knowledgeable, seasoned leadership in marketing, have tried cobbling together teams of youngsters in hopes that they can replace the higher-priced veterans they can no longer find (or afford, if they can find them). This is a major characteristic of the New Economy management structure called *consensus management* or *team management.* Unfortunately, it doesn't usually work; you can add together a dozen brains, and if none of them has the experience, the knowledge, or the vision for the brand, the results from the partnership will be ineffective. In the end, most marketing concepts that emerge by consensus from the work of a team are all too likely to be mainstream, conventional, safe—and mediocre. The concept may work in the boardroom, but it usually fails in the living room.

The next time you notice a truly incompetent new marketing campaign—one you cannot understand, one that damages rather than strengthens the long-term appeal and value of a brand name—you don't need to wonder how on earth it ever got approved. Chaos within our marketing infrastructures is the single greatest cause.

Immunity to Advertising

Advertising clutter is a prominent, inescapable feature of the contemporary scene and a dominant characteristic of both the Old and New Economies. We in business not only have jammed more and more ads into the traditional advertising venues—newspapers and magazines, radio and television—but we are also finding ways to cram ads into spaces that were once ad-free, from grocery shopping carts and school book covers to the lift posts in ski resorts, the urinals in men's rooms and, of course, everybody's Web page. Simultaneously, subtle and not-so-subtle "hidden ads" in the form of product placements have infiltrated movies, TV shows, the print media, theme parks, sports events, concerts—you name it. Even such formerly staid, nonprofit arenas as museums, universities, and public broadcasting are overrun with brand-name promotions (euphemistically called *sponsorships*, of course).

Statistics help capture this ever-growing frenzy to advertise. North American businesses now spend about $170 billion per year on advertising. We air 6000 TV spots a week, up 50 percent from 1983; fully 25 percent of all broadcasting time is now devoted to advertising or on-air promotions. Similarly, about 50 percent of all magazine pages are now filled with advertising, and preprint, flyer pages, and insertions are all up exponentially in the past decade.

Are we enjoying sales results commensurate with all this advertising? You know the answer. At the very time we're jacking up our expenditures on advertising, the results in terms of sales increases and brand loyalty are growing steadily weaker. The problem isn't that our ads are poorly designed or executed; in many surveys, consumers report they find today's TV commercials more entertaining and enjoyable than ever (often more so than the programs they interrupt). The ads are amusing. *But they aren't selling.*

The problem isn't with the idea of advertising or with the ads themselves. The problem is that with a very few exceptions, the underlying marketing strategy no longer works. A once-powerful tool has become impotent.

Increased Reliance on Price Promotions

Faced with the problems of fickle customers, ineffective advertising, and visionless marketing departments, many companies have turned to price promotion as a survival tactic. It's a tried-and-true marketing strategy in many industries, of course, and when used intelligently, price promotions can lure potential customers toward your brand, where its innate value can then hook them for life. At least that's the theory.

The problem is that in today's ultracompetitive business arena, price promotions are now everywhere, often acting not as a supplement to other marketing strategies but as a substitute for them. Businesses have expended a lot of ingenuity in devising ways to grab customers' attention with price-off gimmicks: 50 percent off sales, scratch and win stickers, bonus bucks flyers, you name it. In one sense, the strategy has worked; more and more sales today are predicated on price discounts. In some packaged goods categories, for example, the percentage of products sold on promotion is *double* what it was just a decade ago.

Unfortunately, this strategy isn't a healthy one for a company's long-term survival. For one thing, price promotion doesn't differentiate your product from anyone else's; lowering prices is something anyone can do, so everyone does. It takes no intelligence, no vision, and no customer empathy. Relying on price promotions has a subtly destructive effect on your relationship with your customers. When you offer your product at a reduced price, you are sending several messages—all of them negative: *Our product or service isn't worth paying full price for. When customers pay full price, they're supporting excessive profit margins. All products and services are ultimately the same—the only difference is the price.*

By relying on price promotions, we are telling our customers to believe all these things. And guess what? *Increasingly, throughout the Old and New Economies, they are.*

As a result, more and more industries today are being driven to compete on a price basis. It's happening in newly deregulated industries where price competition was once impossible: Airlines are scrambling for the right to undersell one another on the Internet, and long-distance telephone companies are begging customers to switch providers with the promise that they can save pennies per call. And even upscale goods, from designer clothes and pricey handbags to electronic gadgets and gourmet cookware, are being sold at discount more and more frequently; the outlet-mall price is increasingly viewed as the "normal" price above which no smart customer will go. *We've trained our customers to be a lot smarter about buying than we are about selling.*

Deflation and the Accelerated Product Cycle

There's nothing less appetizing—or less profitable—than a product whose time has passed. At one time, foodstuffs—especially meats—epitomized the perishable. Hence the old saying among butchers, "You either sell it or smell it."

Today, *every* business is turning into a "meat" business. More and more products are becoming perishable, their value short-lived. As a result, not only are businesspeople forced to run faster and faster to keep up with ever-changing consumer demands; they are also finding that their products are rapidly becoming valueless, putting tremendous downward pressure on prices and profits.

One reason is the self-feeding acceleration of technological change. Take the computer business. At one time, this industry featured a predictable, profitable product cycle: When a new technological plateau was reached, a new computer system would be brought to market. For a year or more it would be purchased mainly by "early adapters," people fascinated by the latest gadgetry and willing to pay top dollar for it. Then it would become the industry standard and sell for a couple of years at a slightly lower but still high price, made possible by increased production and its accompanying economies of scale. Finally, with the emergence of a new and improved system, the old system would have a year or more of life as the discounted model, sold to people who didn't need the newest equipment and preferred an older standard, one with all its bugs thoroughly worked out. The cycle allowed manufacturers to rationally plan inventory levels and extract the maximum possible profit from each stage in the product's life. Similar cycles existed in home electronics (from LPs to eight-tracks to cassette players to CDs), appliances, cars, and even (with variations) in such design-driven fashion businesses as clothing and home furnishings.

Today, the predictability of decades past is gone. With new and improved computer chips, software packages, specialized devices, and even monitors and peripherals coming out not once every 2 or 3 years (today, that's a lifetime!) but every few months, the value of inventory in the computer business now dissipates much faster than in the past. The system priced at $2500 today probably will be worth $800 six months from now, when next season's system renders it "obsolete"—and 6 months later, you won't be able to give it away.

To a greater or lesser degree, the same logic of acceleration is afflicting every other business in which new products are driven by technological change. Whether we're talking about "brown goods"—stereos, TVs, VCRs—or "white goods"—refrigerators, ranges, washers, and dryers—innovation is happening faster than ever, and consumers are insisting on the latest array of features with increasing single-mindedness.

The impact of this deflationary pressure is hugely significant to business because the question facing customers is not *whether* to buy but *when* to buy. And because the debate about when to purchase is such an impulse-driven decision, the use of price promotions has become instrumental in shifting historical demand. You can incite customers who have become active buyers to purchase the unit now using price-off tactics. You rarely can incite a nonactive buyer to purchase using price.

Thus the best way to clear out older inventory is to use price to signal to your customer base that has committed to the purchase (but not to its timing) that today would be the best time to buy. By so doing, you have subsidized the purchase and affected its timing, but the longer you hold it, the steeper the incentive necessary to sell it next month might have been.

What if your business deals in the products that aren't technologically based? Don't think you're immune. Within the last decade, the pace and breadth of technological innovation have begun to affect virtually every area of business and life. Take an old-fashioned, low-technology product like the book—a communications medium whose basic nature really hasn't changed in the 500 years since Gutenberg. Book publishers, too, have been caught up in the deflationary impact of accelerated product cycles. How so? Consider a recent short-lived publishing phenomena—the memoirs of Monica Lewinsky. In order to publish Monica's book in a timely fashion—and to have half a chance of recouping the sizable royalty advance the company paid her and her writer, Andrew Morton—Monica's publisher (St. Martin's Press) had to edit, typeset, design, print, manufacture, and distribute her words not in the traditional cycle of 8 or 9 months but in 8 or 9 weeks. *Monica's Story* was one of the increasing number of so-called instant books—a phenomenon first observed some 20 years ago but now far more common than ever before.

How have business and technology trends driven an accelerated product cycle in the staid book industry? In the case of *Monica's Story*, the potential audience for the book—the millions around the world who'd been titillated by the presidential scandal—had been following the story for months not only via the old-fashioned print media—newspapers and magazines—but also electronically, via network and cable TV and the Internet. Each new anecdote, rumor, accusation, and countercharge became known around the world within hours, even minutes, of its initial publication, and the same was true of the revelatory details in Monica's own book. In today's wired world, the shelf life of information is shorter than ever. A Lewinsky memoir published 6 or 8 months after the president's impeachment trial would have had the feeling of ancient history. And all the copies of *Monica's Story* stacked in bookstores that didn't sell within a few weeks were replaced by newer instant books on new topics.

Of course, there are still classic books that sell for years or generations—Shakespeare, Dickens, and the like—just as there are classic styles in fashion that never vanish from the stores completely. But more and more, consumers are demanding that the products they buy reflect only the latest, most up-to-date tastes. Thus, The Gap introduces a completely new line of men's and women's fashions in fresh, up-to-the-minute colors not twice a year *but every 2 months*. Anything slower than this would just not feel current in today's faster-paced world.

All this would be great for business if the success of each new product were guaranteed. Instead, the accelerated product cycle merely increases the financial and creative risk behind every business decision. Books, movies, TV shows, clothing styles, software, fashions in furnishings, consumer electronics, packaged foods and beverages, you name it—all new products now have far less time to establish themselves in the marketplace than they once had. If something doesn't sell in 2 weeks, slash the price and get rid of it—the newer stuff is waiting to take its place.

In this new marketplace, millions can be made *and lost* quicker than ever. Who decides? Not the marketers—they're getting dizzy trying to keep up. The power belongs to the customers—those fickle, demanding, skeptical, distracted millions who've learned to react according to the split-second attention span of the channel-surfer. If they're bored—even for an instant—your business is history.

Declining Profit Margins

As I've already suggested, the technological changes that are driving accelerated product cycles are also driving prices inexorably downward. When everything becomes obsolete quickly, then nothing holds its value; new and better products are continually emerging that are cheaper than the goods already in the system. Consumers know this, and they're willing to pay full price for products only for a fleeting moment at the very start of the product cycle—if then.

Furthermore, we in marketing have educated our customers to *refuse* to pay full price—not only by the overuse of price promotions, as discussed earlier, but also by proliferating outlets where prices are slashed to the bare bones, such as big-box retailers, price clubs, outlet stores, discount catalogues, and Internet auction sites.

The results are predictable. Profit margins in retailing, distribution, and other marketing-oriented businesses were never robust; today they are anemic. Under pressure from Wall Street to justify higher prices for their companies' stocks, marketers are doing whatever they have to do to pump up this quarter's numbers—and to hell with next year. Sometimes this means forcing products out the door in order to reach sales targets—knowing full well they'll come flooding back in the first days of the new fiscal year. Sometimes this means cooking the books to make nonsales register as sales. (One or both of these dubious techniques allegedly were behind the apparent success—and then the ignominious departure—of CEO "Chainsaw Al" Dunlap at Sunbeam. If so, he's only the latest example of a marketer who succumbed to this temptation.)

What makes the current profit squeeze doubly alarming is the fact that North American marketing firms are *not* fat, happy, high-spending enterprises. Just the opposite. For years now, we've been making our profit budgets in the absence of true growth only by reducing expenses, outsourcing services, and trimming staff. We've taken advantage of every possible cost-cutting technique; we've used JIT processes to reduce inventory, we've laid off expensive older employees and replaced them with cheaper, younger ones, and we've eliminated departments devoted to competencies we're not expert at. The employees we've kept are working longer hours than ever, driving productivity up and labor costs down. Our businesses have become lean and mean. Yet profits continue to shrivel. *Something has to give.*

THE MARKETING CREDIBILITY GAP

Every family has a Mom—the person who makes the majority of the financial decisions in the household. In most cases, she is literally "Mom"; millions of households are headed by single women, and even in those families where both a man and woman are present, studies show that the woman generally has the predominant influence not only over purchases of food and clothing but also over decisions about what car or computer to buy and what mutual fund to invest in. (Women buy or influence the purchases of 77 percent of all consumer goods—even menswear, for example.) Thus Mom is the chief financial officer (CFO) of the North American family—the person who drives consumer spending, which, in turns, drives the bulk of the national economy—66 percent of the gross domestic product, to be exact. It's Mom—not Alan Greenspan, Robert Rubin, Bill Gates, or Warren Buffett—who is in charge of our national economic future.

And that's bad news for marketers—because Mom isn't happy with us.

In this respect, as in so many others, the Mom of today is different from her own Mom. A generation ago, in the 1950s, 1960s, and 1970s, we marketers had a system that we thought worked. Within the humming economic engine of postwar North America, we believed that marketing played an important, positive role.

Freed from the burdens of the Great Depression and World War II, and with the burgeoning baby-boom population eager to consume, American corporations turned their creativity to supplying the nation with new and exciting products and services. Marketers added value to the process in a host of ways. They developed a powerful distribution network built around great retail banners—Macy's, Sears, Bloomingdale's—each with a distinctive clientele and merchandise mix. They refined the arts of advertising, especially by means of television, so that powerful selling messages with useful information and real emotional appeal could be delivered to millions of families eager to receive them. Most of all, they built a succession of great brand names, each offering a series of distinctive, high-value products and services whose quality was unique and reliable.

The Moms of the day came to rely on an implicit contract between the marketers and themselves. In effect, this contract said:

- If you patronize the brands we represent, you'll enjoy, at a fair price, the quality we promise. Our reputation is your guarantee.
- If you buy jeans by Levi Strauss, sneakers by Keds, and T-shirts by Fruit-of-the-Loom, you'll dress your kids in clothes that fit well, look good, and last a long time.
- If you launder those clothes using a detergent made by Procter and Gamble, they'll come out clean and fresh every time.
- And if you drive your kids around town in a car built by Ford, General Motors, or Chrysler, you'll enjoy the latest automotive technology made as reliable and affordable as possible.

Millions of North American families accepted these implicit contracts and others like them, and by and large, they got what they bargained for. There was always a degree of cynicism about business, especially about advertising—check out the parodies of commercials in any old issue of *Mad* magazine. On the whole, however, Americans agreed that they could trust American businesses to give them good value for their money—and they proved it by spending billions of dollars supporting and building the world's greatest economic machine. Or so we believed.

Those days are long gone. Today's Mom no longer accepts the old verities her Mom believed. And she certainly hasn't signed on—implicitly or explicitly—to any marketing contract.

It's mainly our fault. Think about what drives your daily business decisions. If you're like most businesspeople, you spend more time thinking about making your boss happy than about making your customers happy. And Mom knows it. Over the years, we've broken many covenants we contracted with her. When our boss needed better margins, we cost-reduced the quality out of the product and researched it to make sure she didn't overtly know it. When we needed sales, we dropped the price of the very product she bought at full retail, not 10 hours earlier.

When we found that remerchandising the store adds valuable sales, we redid the stores, not realizing we added 10 to 25 percent more time to her shopping because she had to relearn where we put everything. And after we sold her this new technology and gave her a help line, she had to wait 40 minutes to get her questions answered.

We enticed her onto the Web, offering better prices and promising a superior shopping experience. Then we hit her with usury charges for shipping and handling at the very end of what was an aggravating, torturously slow online exchange.

We put everything on sale only once each year, then twice, then quarterly, then monthly. Now biweekly. We promised her knowledgeable sales staff and gave her minimally trained children to help her. We build repeat purchases in a product she has learned to trust, and the next thing we do is extend the brand and the product into a proliferation of flavors and sizes and colors and mixtures, most of which don't deliver the original brand experience, all in the name of sales.

We promised to put Mom first—to develop products, services, and Web sites that she would want to use and enjoy. But our actions spoke more loudly than our words. We always seemed to put our shareholders first. Therefore, today, she doesn't believe us any more. We've broken our business contract with her. Today, it's Mom versus marketers. Guess who's winning? She is a far better buyer than we are sellers.

Is Mom buying a car? She'll scrutinize the ads with skepticism and supplement that reading with the latest independent crash tests, ratings from *Consumer Reports*, and government statistics on safety and fuel efficiency. She'll let her local dealer quote her a price on her favorite model—but she'll also cruise the net in search of a competitive offer, even if it saves her only a hundred dollars or so. Today Mom knows exactly what the dealer paid at wholesale and the best time of month to squeeze an extra point or two out of a commission-starved salesperson.

Is Mom shopping for clothes for her kids? Big names still matter—but they're more likely to be the names of sports or movie stars than traditional brands like Levi Strauss and Keds. Or if she wants to save a few bucks, she won't hesitate to snap up the private-label brand at her local discount store—she knows it's every bit as good as the brand-name merchandise (and might even be made at the very same factory).

And when it's laundry time, Mom might choose Tide detergent, just as her Mom did. But she might choose instead whatever brand is on sale for a few cents less in the giant family size at her neighborhood price club store—or spend double the money to buy an "eco-friendly" brand she spots at the health food store.

Mom still wants to buy all these products and many more that didn't even exist a generation ago. The opportunities for businesspeople to sell to her remain. But the predictability, the loyalty, the sense of a contract offered and accepted—all these are gone. Mom still watches the commercials we pay millions of dollars to broadcast on TV. She even enjoys many of them. But she largely ignores them when she makes her buying decisions.

You can see this erosion in the percentage of retail decisions that are preplanned versus in-store. The Point of Purchase Association International (POPAI) has been tracking these numbers for years and has seen a growing influence of in-store marketing on purchase decisions. According to POPAI, the in-store decision rate for packaged goods and grocery items now stands at 70 percent. For mass merchandisers or discounters, the number is 74 percent.

What further proof do we need to understand that our promises, enticements, and lives have become irrelevant to Mom? What more do we need to realize that traditional marketing has become impotent to affect customer demand?

WHY MARKETING IMPOTENCE?

Once upon a time, not so very long ago, marketers knew how to deliver customers and could do so reliably and profitably. No more.

Marketing has become impotent.

It didn't happen quickly, like a sudden heart attack that fells a seemingly robust person. It was more like a cancer, slowly yet inexorably eating away profits, the way cancer cells gradually leach energy from the healthy cells nearby.

To understand what happened, you need to know the *marketing equation:*

$$\text{Brand value} = \frac{\text{equity}}{\text{price}}$$

This is a deceptively simple but revealing formula. *Brand value* is what your product or service is worth, as perceived by customers. *Price* is, simply, what it costs. The difference between the two is *equity.* And the real purpose of marketing—though few people, even in business, fully understand this—is to *build brand equity*—to constantly support, strengthen, and increase the perceived equity in the brands you serve. This is what the world's best marketing companies focus on, and from their efforts emerge the great brand names businesspeople admire and customers covet: Coca-Cola, Nike, Sony, Charles Schwab, Home Depot, the New York Yankees, Microsoft, and others.

Think of equity as the *worthiness* of the brand in the eyes of the customer. Of course, worthiness may mean different things to different people. Sometimes worthiness is based on the physical attributes of a brand—the safety of Mom's favorite brand of sports utility vehicle, for instance; sometimes it's based on the emotional qualities the brand conveys—the association of L'Oreal hair products with glamour and prestige, for example ("Because I'm worth it"). Whatever its source, worthiness is always measured by the premium that Mom is willing to pay for the brand over its lowest-cost competitor.

Here's another way to think about equity. Imagine if I were to purchase all the assets of the Coca-Cola Company—all its office buildings, equipment, factories, delivery trucks, and even the famous "secret formula" for Classic Coke—all the assets, that is, *except for its brand name*. I could use those assets to begin producing, marketing, and selling my own cola drink. It would be identical to today's Coca-Cola, except for its brand name—let's call it Chick-Cola. (I used to know a guy named Chick who always dreamed of owning his own soda company. This one's for you, Chick.)

Now, would the sales of Chick-Cola be the same as the sales of Coca-Cola? Would the new Chick-Cola Company be worth as much as the old Coca-Cola Company? You know the answer to both questions: No way. Nobody has heard of Chick-Cola; it's a name that stands for nothing, conjures up no positive images, captures no memories, stimulates no taste buds. I'd sell a few cases, sure, but it would take decades for my new company to build sales that would even make it onto the Nielsen Report for Coke.

Remember, in this experiment, Chick-Cola now owns all the assets of Coca-Cola, with the sole exception of the great brand name. Yet its value as a business is much, much less. *What makes the difference is brand equity.*

The greater the perceived equity in a product or service, the greater the brand value—and the more you can demand for the product or service. By contrast, when marketing doesn't work, there is little perceived value, and customers demand lower prices. The inevitable result is ever-shrinking margins and ever-increasing profit pressure. Today's marketing impotence is caused by the fact that, in most industries, the marketing tools are incapable of increasing worthiness. And as worthiness decreases, the price you can demand for the product or service, by definition, will decrease faster. The inevitable result is a deadly, downward spiral in profits. In today's rapidly changing business environment, this fate is enveloping more and more companies—even some of those responsible for the greatest brands in the world.

This is a critical issue. Had business not abandoned marketing in the Old Economy, the relationship between brands and customers would have evolved differently. Look at the European market, where brand stewardship is a career and marketers are judged by the continued quality of the brand franchise. In these markets, price is not the driving force it is in North America. Instead, brand value is focused on the equity of the brand. As a result, the European *Maman* has been more willing than the American Mom to pay a fair market price that supports the quality of their brands.

Because North American companies used up much of the brand equity to build sales, when the New Economy hit us, the predominant consumer model used was low price and free access. The Web didn't come out of the box in the B2C space as a value enhancer but as an extension of the destructive emphasis on lower prices, thereby continuing and accelerating the inability of North American businesses to compete profitably. Only now, as we come to the opening of 2002, is the Web refocusing on adding value rather than reducing costs, and as a result, subscription-based models are beginning to succeed.

Success in the Next Economy cannot come from the use of Old Economy marketing tools. They are impotent at affecting consumer sales and are destructive to corporate profits.

Is there a solution? Of course. It lies in developing new tools for building equity—tools adapted to the new marketing environment we find ourselves in at the start of the new millennium. The traditional values we've been offering Mom since the 1950s just don't work any longer. However, a new set of tools, core competencies for the coming decade, holds out the promise of creating a new marketing contract with the American customer—one that's as meaningful to tomorrow's Moms as the old contract was to their mothers.

In the Old Economy, what you sold defined who you were. You were the shoe store, the drug store, the department store, the food store. But because of the inability to satisfy customer demand in the products that defined the business and the subsequent price erosion that dried up profits, a relentless chase for additional, more profitable product lines led to the erosion in customer confidence as retailers increasingly turned themselves into general stores from specialty shops.

In the New Economy, nobody measured profitability. We developed new measurements of success—eyeballs, traction, stickiness—none of which were intended to measure customer satisfaction. *How* you sold defined who you were; you were a pure play, a hybrid, or a bricks-and-mortar business. What you sold mattered least. Business growth was based on your business model, your space, and your click-through rate.

In the Next Economy, *who* you sell will define who you are. The type of customer you capture will define what and how you sell her.

Your ability to become a relevant part of her life will drive your business, and her loyalty will become the single most important measurement of your success.

Unfortunately, the time to act is short. As I suggested in the first few pages of this chapter, the symptoms we observe in today's businesses are only precursors of the still more dramatic, dangerous changes that lie ahead. The social and economic forces that have produced the dilemmas today's marketers face are continuing to gather strength. They'll crest in the early years of the new century. To fully grasp the upheaval ahead and the significant steps we have to take to survive it, you need to understand its larger causes. I will address that topic in the pages that follow.

3

The Rise of Customer Power

Whe are witnessing today the latest phase of a long-term historic trend—a gradual shift in power between segments of our economy. In many ways, the advent of the Internet represents its culmination. Unless we in business understand this shift, we'll be unable to respond effectively in the Next Economy.

The rise of the Next Economy is fundamentally possible because of three major colliding realities:

- The shift of power from the business to the customer
- The changing economic priorities of the baby-boomer population
- The availability of technology to facilitate and accelerate the first two changes

Without all three trends developing and intersecting in North America sometime in the second half of the first decade of the twenty-first century, the Next Economy would not be. But these three undeniable trends are sure to collide and explode. The question isn't *if*, only *when*.

ECONOMICS, FROM THE SUPPLY SIDE TO THE DEMAND SIDE

The first of the three key trends, the shift of power from the business to the customer, is actually the culmination of a 200-year-old evolution. In the 1700s, the importer held the greatest share of marketing power in the North American economy—that is, the ability to influence what's in the cupboards and closets of customers. Importers would go to Europe, consign goods, and bring them back by ship; North American customers had no choice but to pick from the goods the importers had chosen.

By around 1850, the manufacturer had the greatest share of marketing power. The manufacturing base had developed in North America, and small producers were springing up everywhere. These producers in large measure decided what America would buy; the goods they made were carried across the continent by traveling salespeople, and customers in the scattered cities, towns, and rural outposts bought what was available.

In the 1950s, the center of marketing power shifted to retailers. The concept of bringing the store to the community—a brilliant innovation in its day—gave retailers control; it was the great age of shopping centers and department store chains. As the last link in the chain from manufacturer to customer, the retailers "owned" the customers, who made their buying decisions under the guidance of the ads, displays, and sales of local merchants.

Today, the power center is moving again, due both to technology and to social changes. *Within the next 10 years, the customer will hold all the controlling cards in the economy.*

There are several main causes of this new shift.

THE COMING DEMOGRAPHIC SHAKEUP

As we all realize, the huge baby-boom generation repeatedly has reshaped the United States and the world—socially, psychologically, politically, and economically. Although in this book we are most concerned with the effect the baby boomers have had on the economy through their purchasing behavior, in reality, all these effects are closely interwoven.

The impact of the baby boomers was first felt back in the 1960s, when millions of baby boomers were in their late teens and early twenties. Thanks to the explosion of youth culture not only in the United States but also in western Europe and other countries, the baby boomers generated long-lasting changes in dress, music, politics, values, and social structures.

They initiated a value change in society that shocked the system. Fueled by their numbers, they rebelled against mindless acceptance of authority and instilled a concept that the system could be changed if enough people believed in the change. This was a major paradigm shift. Prior to the 1960s, most sons wanted to be like their fathers, most daughters like their moms. If Dad drove a Chevy, you drove a Chevy. If Mom used Ivory soap, you did too.

The rebellious 1960s changed all this. If Dad drove a Chevy, you drove anything but a Chevy. If Mom used Ivory soap, you used anything *but* Ivory soap. Better still, you used nothing at all.

The baby-boomer generation took the evolutionary concept of household branding and destroyed it in one 10-year period. Long-standing household brands disappeared from the shelves. New ones based on very different values took their place.

In the 1970s, the idealists, protestors, students, and hippies of the 1960s "morphed" into the "me generation." As they left school, launched families, and created their own homes, the baby boomers spent their money quite differently from previous generations.

The "me generation" saw goods and services as an extension and representation of their value structure. In the past, this was true mainly of prestigious products. In the 1970s, the individualism born in the 1960s became an economic phenomenon as baby boomers dressed according to their own code, using their fashions and wanting their brands not because they were expensive but because they were different. As the 1970s spilled over into the 1980s, specialty stores proliferated, which drove the need for ever-more, ever-bigger shopping centers. Stores catering to different niches evolved and multiplied. Fashion was no longer just a look; it was an expression of how you personalized what you wore. And for a time, music said it all.

In the 1980s, the baby boomers metamorphosed again. Entering their thirties, the baby boomers had begun to settle into their working careers. Many members of this well-educated generation became business professionals, technical experts, or managers. And due to the liberalized equality that characterized the 1960s, millions of women entered the workforce, founding affluent double-income households and delaying child rearing. The result was an unprecedented surge in disposable income, and sure enough, as the decade wore on, the baby boomers began to spend like no generation before them. The 1980s turned into a decade of decadence, highlighted by enormous consumption and the disposability of everything from products to homes to careers to marriages.

All of this was hard to believe from a generation that only 20 years earlier had rejected most icons of acceptance and success. Nonetheless, the spending boom of the 1980s once again altered the economy in a dramatic way as premium products soared, convenience ruled, and designer brands became mass products available to the burgeoning, affluent middle class.

In the 1990s, the baby boomers began to turn 40, and another series of psychological adjustments kicked in. The realization that you have probably lived more than half your productive life has an impact on what you do with your money. Entering middle age, the baby boomers began to realize that they would have to make provisions for their future—and with the well-publicized problems of the Social Security system (greatly exacerbated by the huge size of the baby-boomer generation), many feared that the government couldn't be counted on. So millions of baby boomers began investing. And as they did so, they reinvented investing on their own terms, just as they reinvented everything. Stock ownership exploded. As a result, over 50 percent of American households now own stocks in some form (including mutual funds), a far greater percentage than ever before.

Did they stop spending? Nope. They drove personal debt to new highs as they financed their acquisition of goods and services, using their liquidity to continue to invest in the market.

Now we're in the first decade of the twenty-first century (which I call "the naughts"), and the baby boomers are reaching 50. The impact of this transition over the next decade will be huge. As the Dent spending curve shows (Figure 3-1), there's a predictable pattern to individual spending by age, and the baby boomers are now in their peak spending period, which occurs when the head of the household is between the ages of 45 and 55. After that, for most households, spending starts to decrease. By age 55, most people have acquired pretty much everything they want; their kids grow up and move out, and many people consider moving to smaller living quarters and perhaps working less. In short,

Figure 3-1 The Dent curve: Key consumer expenditures/investments by age.

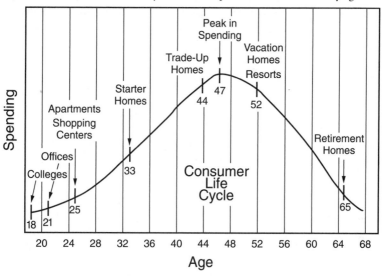

Source: Adapted from Harry S. Dent, Jr., *The Roaring 2000's Investor*, Simon & Schuster, 1999. Reprinted by permission.

they begin to be more discerning and selective in their spending and to withdraw from the marketplace.

Lest you minimize the impact of this baby-boomer value change on the economy, remember how radically different each of the preceding decades were as the baby boomers' demographic mouse worked its way up the economic snake. The "protesting" 1960s, the "me generation" 1970s, the "shop-till-you-drop" 1980s, and the "investment" 1990s were all shocks to the economic system. I've labeled the naughts the *decade of solitude*, as baby boomers begin their withdrawal from traditional spending patterns and start to focus on savings and investing instead.

Ask any retired person and you'll find out that his or her two critical concerns are good health and enough money. These two preoccupations will draw liquidity from the retail marketplace. Ironically, this focus on savings instead of spending will have a huge negative impact on the financial markets. The slowing of retail sales will drive stock prices downward, and this, in turn, will further dry up spending by the stock-market-loving baby boomers. The Federal Reserve (Fed) cannot stop this negative spiral because lowering the interest rates only works if there is demand for goods and services. If there's little to finance the Fed's leverage on consumers, its impact on the downturn will be minimal.

Even as far back as 1998, organizations and individuals who study the impact of demographics on consumption came to the conclusion that retail spending will soften in the middle of the naughts. A study by Richard K. Green, cited in *Chain Store Age* in May of 1998, forecast a 30-year draught before retail growth was reestablished (Figure 3-2).

We already have major business upheavals today, in a +3 to +6 percent market. What do you think will happen in a −5 percent reality? The prospects are downright alarming.

As I write (in late-2001), the economy is experiencing its first slowdown in a decade. In fact, I think this is merely a precursor of the major restructuring that will follow when the largest portion of the babyboomer generation as whole enters the period of withdrawal. We probably can expect another 3 or 4 years of acceptable spending in most sectors of the economy. However, by 2005–2006, we'll start to feel the withdrawal. *A major societal redefinition of what people buy and how they buy it is in store.* It'll be a very dangerous time for the North American economy.

BIRTH OF THE SMART CONSUMER

Today's customers are better educated and understand how to buy better than ever before. Thus they are in a position to demand and wield greater power than previous generations of customers.

Figure 3-2 What will happen in a −5 percent retail reality? Projected change in U.S. per capita spending.

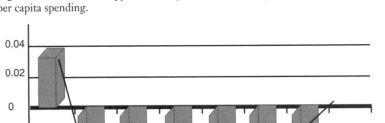

Source: Chain Store Age, May 1998. Reprinted by permission.

Out of the two-thirds of the gross domestic product (GDP) that is fueled by consumer spending, over three-quarters is purchased directly by women or significantly influenced by women. And today's Mom, the chief financial officer (CFO) of the American household, has become a much smarter buyer than we are sellers. She is better educated than past generations and has at her disposal far more tools for smart consumption than were ever available in the past—magazines, newspaper columns, TV and radio features on consumer news, and of course, the ubiquitous Internet.

Furthermore, Mom now has less time than her counterpart of a generation ago; she often works at least one job outside the home while continuing to be deeply involved in caring for her spouse and kids. Therefore, she's more time-pressured and driven to use her time and money wisely. She's smart enough to know when the value is right and perfectly prepared to wait until it is. She's learned to build household inventory when prices are slashed. She buys a majority of her goods and services on deal. She has no time to shop but finds plenty of time to return stuff we misrepresented to her. She's learned to combine buying power with that of her friends to get even better savings. She's much more patient than we are. She knows that fashion cycles demand markdowns, that prices drop late in any seasonal product, and that every merchant will match a legitimately lower competitive price.

Traditionally, marketing was defined as managing the flow of goods and services from the supplier to the customer. No more. Today, marketing is a response to the customer. More than ever, we in business will have to cater to the customer in terms of the physiology of the purchase (i.e., the physical factors of the shopping experience) as well as the psychology of the buying experience. If we don't, Mom is gone. And so are we.

ABUSING THE CUSTOMER RELATIONSHIP

Here's a truth most businesses would rather not face: *Most women (and men) don't really like to shop any longer.* Although we businesspeople like to claim that they do—that a visit to the mall is high on most Moms' priority lists—the research I've seen shows that this is simply not the case. Today's women are simply too busy to enjoy shopping, especially the way we've arranged the experience.

As a result, most customers complain to one another (and to us, if we're willing to listen) about how badly we've mangled our jobs and unnecessarily complicated their lives. They complain about how goods are scattered throughout the mall rather than clustered by category (the way food is clustered in a mall). They complain about the proliferation of look-alike styles in every store. They complain about poorly trained and ill-equipped sales staffs. All in all, the job of procuring clothes, housewares, furniture, electronic gadgets—you name it—is no fun.

Mom is fed up and has rebelled. She has driven profitability to new lows by telling us that price is the only component in the marketing mix that she respects. Everything else we try to tell her and teach her seemingly falls on deaf ears.

BUYERS' MARKET

Another reason for the rise in the customer's power is increased competition among sellers. When competition among sellers is intense, what results is a buyers' market. *Today's emerging reality is the greatest buyers' market in history.*

We are terribly overstored. Retail space per capita keeps growing. Add to this the Internet's ability to search for stock keeping units (SKUs) by price point, and you have an array of e-tail/retail merchants trying to undercut each other while competing for the transaction. We aren't talking profits but simply the transaction itself that turns inventory and generates an open invitation to buy.

Our inability to source unique products or provide large-scale personalized service, whether online or in-store, has turned much of what America consumes into commodities. Travel down the interstate highway for a few days and you're struck by the repetitiousness of the service offerings off every exit. Drop by three or four suburban malls and try to find a unique mix of stores. Go online and search for a given brand. You'll be amazed at how many retailers there are to choose from and how little choice each provides.

There are many causes for this glut of competition. Some of the causes grow out of global economics. As rapidly developing countries such as Singapore, Chile, Malaysia, Indonesia, Brazil, and Korea, as well as the nations of the former Soviet bloc, such as Poland, Hungary, Romania, Russia, and the Czech Republic, ramp up their industrial capacities and join more fully in the free-market economy, products from these countries find their way to other marketplaces around the world.

Traditional barriers are also falling internally. Businesses of all types are now selling all kinds of merchandise. All retailers have become, to a large extent, general stores. You can buy a television from a drug store, a superstore, a club store, a department store, a discount store, a catalog store, or a shopping channel. You can buy it online or in any flea market anywhere in North America. And that's a *new* TV!

TECHNOLOGY AND THE TRANSACTION

The final reason for the growth of customer power is technology. The New Economy didn't last long, but its input on consumption and buying behavior will stand for centuries. The information era made one outstanding change to relationships among merchants, manufacturers, and their customers. *It reversed the historical interaction between parties by putting the seller at the beck and call of the buyer.*

Ever since the traveling salesman died, customers have had to buy from the place where merchants and manufacturers choose to sell. While greatly inconveniencing us, the argument was that the trip was worth the time and effort. To continue to entice customers out of their comfortable chairs, retailers built bigger stores and added more merchandise. Malls put in specialty stores between the anchors. Car dealers opened up together in their "golden mile."

The Web changed all this forever. In a short time period, vendors had to revert to the old days by lining up at the customer's house once again, this time in virtual reality. Unfortunately, most of the chief executive officers (CEOs) of the dotcom community weren't old enough to remember the high-caliber service that historically came with the Fuller Brush man.

Nevertheless, the power to bring together multiple organizations all competing for a single transaction, all controlled by the customer, was a crushing reversal of 40 years of transaction evolution. It singularly shifted the balance of power to the customer and laid another stone of the foundation on which the Next Economy will be built.

THE 5-YEAR DECLINE IN BRAND LOYALTY

As a result of all the preceding trends, products and services have become increasingly substitutable in the customer's mind. There are fewer and fewer unique selling propositions. In most product categories, there's no longer enough distinctiveness to warrant any significant price differentiation. In the minds of more and more customers, several brands are equally acceptable—a slap in the face to marketing and the theory of marketing. Thus the relationship with the brand has changed—the product may no longer be in the pantry every week, interacting with the consumer, and therefore, it's no longer part of the family. Take a look at the chart in Figure 3-3. It not only defines this loyalty drop, but it also brings several related issues to mind. First, this is a loyalty check for well-known brands. Second, the largest dropoff rate occurs with baby boomers aged 37–55. The impact on branding is that the baby boomers don't feel the same degree of loyalty as their parents did about which brand they choose.

The reasons for this trend are numerous. I believe it started in the 1960s and 1970s when store labels duplicated as closely as legally possible the graphics and look of the leading brands in several high-volume categories. As many people began experimenting with these store brands, they learned that seemingly lower-quality product at significant savings was an acceptable alternative. As the store-brand label strategy changed in the 1980s and 1990s to replicating and sometimes exceeding the quality of the brand-category leaders, the concept of experimenting with lesser-known brands and getting comparable quality became more broadly accepted.

The inability of brand leaders to maintain their distinctiveness in packaging, technology, and distribution led Mom to believe that a short list of brands was acceptable to her family and that the brand she chose

Figure 3-3 Percentage of customers who say they stick to well-known brands.

Age	1975	1985	1995	2000
20–29	66%	57%	50%	59%
30–39	73	55	55	59
40–49	77	59	53	60
50–59	82	65	62	59
60–69	86	69	62	65
70–79	93	78	72	73

Source: David J. Lipke, "Pledge of Alliance, DDB Lifestyle Study 2000, cited in American Demographics, November 2000.

could be based primarily on price. This desire for experimentation, seeded in the rebellious 1960s as a value structure, began showing up in the 1980s and 1990s, and brand loyalty took a kicking.

Today, whether or not it's a result of the rapidity with which technology can now spread ideas and product designs, the sameness of retail, or the widespread availability of risk-free guarantees, manufacturers rarely can produce uniqueness any more, certainly not in the business-to-customer (B2C) sphere. The few points of differentiation that still exist are so removed from the customer's value structure that they are irrelevant to him or her. As a result, price is becoming the only deciding factor in most purchase decisions.

CAN MARKETERS SURVIVE?

As we've seen, the rise of the all-powerful customer is the logical culmination of an economic process that has been under way for two centuries. Among other consequences, this means that the day of the intermediary is fading rapidly—the phenomenon known as *disintermediation*. If marketers—the intermediaries par excellence—hope to remain relevant, they must find new ways to add value to the buying experience for their customers.

And they must move quickly. The trends that are causing this series of changes are not refutable, and they are macro trends rather than micro trends. This is why these trends are unstoppable and why marketing must be reinvented—and soon.

4

The Failure of the Four P's

The vast majority of companies attempting to make their profits from the consumer segment of the economy are having serious problems delivering their bottom-line numbers consistently. The evolution from the Old Economy to the New Economy to the Next Economy has left such companies with an antiquated set of tools that do not work any longer. As a result, the symptoms described in the last two chapters are all too familiar to a number of corporations. This new reality, coupled with the rise in customer power, has left many corporations wondering how to effectively reinvent their businesses.

At the core of the problem is marketing impotence, a problem that business has yet to acknowledge. Over the past 40 years, since the baby boomers started their cultural revolution of the 1960s, corporations that cater to consumers have reinvented literally every aspect of their business except marketing. Marketers, ironically charged with being ahead of consumer trends, have steadfastly refused to acknowledge the symptoms described in Chapter 2 or the impact on their business of the rise in customer power. They continue to practice a trade using tools that no longer work.

The truth is that the traditional Four P's of marketing—Price, Product, Place, and Promotion—on which all marketing strategy is built, are no longer capable of affecting customer behavior. It's time to reinvent marketing for the Next Economy.

You recall the brand value equation:

$$\text{Brand value} = \frac{\text{equity}}{\text{price}}$$

In the Old Economy and even in the New Economy, the right side of this equation was made up of the four traditional elements called the Four P's:

$$\text{Brand value} = \frac{\text{Product} + \text{Place} + \text{Promotion}}{\text{Price}}$$

For generations, marketers have been taught the Four P's as the basis of their discipline. Under this doctrine, the definition of brand value grew naturally out of the old definition of marketing. This definition stated that *marketing* is the management of the flow of goods and services from the manufacturer to the consumer. Under this definition, marketing was focused on two things: *what's for sale* and *how to sell it*.

Now this must change. In the Next Economy, the focus of marketing will shift from *what's for sale* and *how to sell* it to *why they buy*.

At one time, the Four P's worked reasonably well to define what marketers needed to focus on. This is no longer true. One of the major causes of marketing impotence is the failure of the Four P's to relate to customers in a meaningful way.

Let's consider each of the Four P's and how it has lost its power to connect to consumers on behalf of your brand.

THE FIRST P: PRODUCT

The Death of the USP

Manufacturers used to offer differentiated products. Twenty-five years ago, the ultimate measurement of a good marketer was the ability to define a unique selling proposition (USP) for the customer base. It was all based on the idea that different manufacturing technologies could justify differentiated price and thereby add measurable value to the brand. Again, notice the focus: What's for sale? The job of the marketer was to say, "Here's what we sell and how it's different."

This is not true any more. As we've seen, Point of Purchase Association International (POPAI) data show that people are making most of their purchasing decisions in the store rather than before shopping. It means that people are no longer going into the store locked on a particular brand. Instead, they're short-list shopping, readily buying any of a handful of acceptable products, because they no longer believe that product differentiation justifies a price premium.

There are several reasons why product has become an insignificant factor in brand value. Technology now lets us duplicate products very quickly. Duplicating fashion styles as well as other product types is very easy now. Anything that's available in London, Milan, Munich, or Tokyo is known about immediately and imitated and duplicated, often within a few weeks. As a result, while business used to be a product developers game, it's now a mercenary's game. True, whoever has the most money gets new technology first, but lead times are measured in weeks, not years.

I remember when a breakthrough formula for a substance known as alpha-hydroxy acid became a big deal in the cosmetics industry. I was working with Revlon in Canada at the time. It looked like technology had finally delivered a truly revolutionary cosmetic product that was going to make a physical difference to women's appearance—and give Revlon a long-term product advantage. By the time I had the launch strategy approved, however, every single competitor had its own version ready to go. It became an advertising war rather than a product war.

Another reason: Much of research and development is now being outsourced. We see this in food companies, drug companies, and above all in the makers of all kinds of private-label packaged goods. The trend is driven by the demands manufacturers face to lower costs and raise stock prices. There's nothing wrong with outsourcing in itself, but when something as fundamental as the development of new products is divorced from the company, the distinctiveness and heritage of the product can be lost. The outside research and product design company may have no understanding of the intimate relationship between the customer and the brand.

Remember that the customer relationship is with the brand, not with the company. The product or service represents that relationship. However, the brand is why the corporation can get a premium. Outsourcing product development to people who may not have an intimate understanding of the historical relationship between the customer and the brand puts into jeopardy this relationship because its stewardship is passed to people who are product-driven, not customer-driven.

This problem with product development can exist just as easily within a corporation. You see brand extensions into product categories that have little relationship to the parent brand but are simply opportunities to get shelf space or fill a distribution channel with short-term sales. How many different products can be licensed before deleting the brand equity? How many sizes, shapes, colors, and packages can a brand be extended to before the customer questions its integrity? When does the customer contract get broken?

Examples of companies that have won or lost because of their respect for the connection between the product and the customer are easy to find. For decades, Kraft's success was built on the consistency of its "hands and recipes" campaigns. For years, Kraft told its customers that if its name wasn't on the product, Kraft didn't make it. It was a blatant reference to the practice of food retailers of duplicating packaging and product presentation in their store-label programs. "We don't play that game," the people at Kraft said. And the company continually developed recipes and presented them in the advertising, offering new and easy ways for Mom to use the product.

This simple set of messages was communicated consistently for years and was wonderfully effective at separating Kraft from its competitors. In my opinion, this heritage was lost for decades and only recently is starting to come back. The company's future success will hinge in large part on whether or not it can recapture the credibility it enjoyed historically.

For decades, the great car companies were good at nurturing the relationship between the product and the customer. A few still understand what's needed. The new Jaguar and its evolution from the Jaguar tradition of the 1950s and 1960s is a good example.

By contrast, the caretakers of the General Motors Oldsmobile brand never respected the heritage of the brand. In the mid-1980s, attempting to modernize its image, they used the advertising line, "This is not your father's Oldsmobile." In doing so, I believe they denigrated Oldsmobile's own image and heritage. This misstep started a series of brand-stewardship mistakes, including the creation of new models with little or no corporate identification at all. The managers at Oldsmobile might as well have started a whole new car company. In the end, they wound up with nothing.

As the Oldsmobile story suggests, *attempting to overhaul a brand— especially based on the four P's—almost always leads to losing customers faster than you gain them.*

The Temptation of Private Labels

As the Kraft example illustrates, retail private labeling has been another cause of the death of product. When your customer becomes your biggest competitor, you have a huge problem, and this is exactly what happened in many categories during the 1970s and 1980s as supermarkets, department stores, and other retailers developed private-label product lines to compete with those offered by their vendors.

The branded-label companies then compounded the problem. They refused to recognize that the private-label brands looked and felt the same as their own products. As a result, they failed to fight back by taking a stand against those who imitated their packaging. They were playing Russian roulette—toying with brand suicide.

We already know that in-store decision making comprises a large proportion of shopping behavior. It's a critical point of contact with customers. If product packaging is developed that is close enough to the leading brands' color and font style so that customers either believe it to be the brand leader or more likely believe it is made by the brand leader, they may be more likely to buy it. And if, on trying it, the product delivers consumer expectations at less cost, the concept of product as a valuable asset in building brand value has once again failed marketers.

When the store brands became common, manufacturers were unable to differentiate their own brands from the store brands. Many private-label goods were made in the same factories as the branded products, often with the only difference being the packaging. This problem was inevitable, given the cost structure of most companies and the role to which marketing was relegated—after all, brand managers do not control operations, so they couldn't stop this kind of copycat manufacturing from happening.

Look down any aisle of any grocery store. Look through the basics of any department store. Explore the product similarities in any drug store. You will be surprised to find the similarities between leading brands in a given category of merchandise and the store brand competitive offering. All of this supports the consumer perception that product is easily substituted and that price should be the governing criterion in making any purchase decision.

The leading brands should have used their leverage as a group to prevent the kind of close imitation that has occurred. However, the kind of product volume opportunity presented by the private-label products was very tempting. In an oligopoly, where just four or five brands dominate the majority of a category's sales, being the low-cost producer is a huge competitive advantage. This is so because oligopolists usually have large fixed overhead costs that determine their profitability. A major contract to supply store brands significantly contributes to eating up that overhead. This drives the breakeven point down and profitability up.

Unfortunately, marketers have no control over these decisions. Operations and sales divisions drive store-brand policy and derive the benefits of a successful private-label strategy. Ironically, the more successful the operations people are at running at full capacity using store-brand volume, the more vulnerable the corporation becomes. Its branded franchise corrodes, while the lower cost becomes built into forward projections. When the store-brand contract comes up for renewal, most of these vendors have no choice but to renew. This provides the retailer with an extraordinary negotiating advantage, which in turns costs the manufacturer margin. The cycle then begins to spiral downward as reduced margins affect profitability, which affects marketing funds available to support the company's brands, which further erodes the customer franchise into a commodity. Not a pretty scenario but fairly common.

A manufacturer always must protect the essence of the product experience. Never forget: Manage the contact points between the customer and your brand. They include the visual moment of recognition on the store shelf as well as the physical preparation and use of the product. Consider these points of contact holy—that's how crucial they are.

THE SECOND P: PLACE

The End of Expertise

Place was once critical in differentiating brands. Where you bought something affected your relationship with the brand. It dignified the price structure or justified the expectation of cost.

Back then, distribution, or "place," meant expertise. Even as recently as the 1970s and 1980s, we relied on the sales associates for information. The salesperson gave us information, and then we gave the store our business. The expertise salespeople provided also carried extra profit margins for everyone.

Today, in an effort to keep labor costs reasonable, part-time associates, call-center operators, and delivery people are more prevalent than ever. Once again, at the point of customer contact, we have replaced experience and knowledge with enthusiasm and politeness. Whether it's a Web site or a store, our most valuable asset, Mom, comes in contact daily with individuals who know little about her request.

The problem is made more critical because of the proliferation of stock keeping unit (SKUs) many retailers now carry. Thus, keeping up with broadening inventory categories is a challenge. So too are technology changes. Each year new appliances and home electronics products flood the marketplace. How can even a seasoned professional, let alone a part-time student, keep up with the array of new features and specs? It's an almost impossible task.

The New Economy has further added to the problem with expertise. If the information era did anything right, it was to accumulate a ton of data on everything. Avid potential buyers of technology could and still can research the specifications, comparison shop online, and if they choose, walk into any retailer better informed and more knowledgeable than those supposed experts who would serve them.

There have been many attempts at trying to solve the dilemma of expertise and its demise in the customer transaction. Home Depot has hired a slew of retired craftspeople to help build expertise on the floor. Wal-Mart started the greeter phenomenon to help at least thank customers for coming. Some retailers have changed their compensation method, putting sales associates on commission in the hope that this would help initiate a proactive approach to floor selling. But most corporations that deal directly with the customer agree that at the point of transaction they are woefully underrepresented in talent and expertise. They further agree that training will become the single, most critical expense as they attempt to rebuild credibility. They may run out of time!

Customers still need and want expertise. If anything, today's products are more specialized, complicated, and advanced than those of the past, not less so. However, retailers are no longer in a position to provide expertise. And the consumer goods manufacturers no longer have budgets with which to support the retailers. Once they had people on the road working on the floors to train salespeople. As a result, stores had some knowledge they could apply to help customers; if you had problems with a ski, you could get help from the retailer. This expertise is gone. If you need help today, you'll look for it on the Internet—not at the retail level. You'll spend half a day waiting for the tech support department to respond to your question and another half a day figuring out its answer.

Buying Everything Everywhere

At one time, place also meant convenience. You gave your business to the local retailer because he or she was convenient—if necessary, you could return the product easily. Convenience is now much less of a factor because of the sophistication of delivery systems. Sears Canada, for example, can get your product shipped to the closest of 3500 independent dealers across the nation or to the closest Sears retail store. And UPS or Fedex can pick up a package for return overnight.

Today, there's a Radio Shack within 5 minutes of 94 percent of the U.S. population. And the ultimate convenience is the Web, where in the comfort of your home you can access the world of e-tail and order anything you wish, have it delivered overnight, and return it the day after if you don't like it. Convenience is no longer a differentiating attribute of Place. You can now buy anything anywhere.

So Place is not going to help you build brand value nor brand equity. Yet we all acknowledge that the core value that Place historically brought to the marketplace was expertise. This expertise issue will have to be reinvented in the Next Economy, where expertise will be sought by an information-saturated customer desperately seeking real knowledge in the form of objective advice and help in choosing and using the product.

THE THIRD P: PROMOTION

The Trouble with Advertising

Somewhere along the way between the Old Economy and the New Economy, business lost sight of the fact that the role of advertising was to inform consumers about the unique mix of product or service attributes and distinctiveness that differentiated its brand from those of the competition. After all, advertising has never been more than a promise. What it has always done is give visible form to the invisible contract that the brand offers its potential customers.

The problem is that as the uniqueness of the offering disappeared, the ability to differentiate one brand from another also disappeared. Since the advertising industry is a well-connected and critical part of the customer relationship, to continue this role, marketers decided that if they had nothing different to say to their customers, they would at least say it differently.

Today, our advertising is better differentiated than our brands. And while awareness of advertising moves up, brand loyalty is in decline. One of the key issues here is the role of advertising as the catalyst for trial. If advertising is a promise, its purpose should be to set an expectation that is deliverable by the brand—to give the consumer contract meaning, to set the criteria for judgment.

The second role of advertising is to ensure that the awareness of the campaign gets transferred to the brand to result in trial. If there is no transfer of the awareness, there is no trial. However, when we see ad recall moving up and ad-sales ratios static, we know that this is not happening. The ads may be entertaining and memorable. They may break through the clutter. But they are not doing what brand management needs them to do—stimulate trial. This is why Starch scores have often generated huge "noted" numbers, small "associated" numbers, and minimal "read most" numbers. The customer recognizes the ad, fails to associate with the folks paying for it, and doesn't recall the body text that was supposed to differentiate the brand from its competition.

For years I've heard creative people complain about how their work gets compromised by their clients. I've watched directors' reels of commercials that they are proud of and are very different from the cut the client approved and aired. This changed in the New Economy. The New Economy was run by 20- and 30-year-old chief executive officers (CEOs) who loved creativity. Finally, creative got through, unscathed by the client Philistines. The result? Total confusion. No contact was established. In many cases, the advertising conveyed no idea as to what the hell it was selling. Millions of dollars were spent. Where are those brands today—EToys, iVillage, DrKoop, and all the other big spenders in the New Economy? Most are dead or dying.

Nonetheless, advertising agencies continue to turn out bright, creative ideas that fail to encourage trial or repeat purchasing. The marketing community refuses to recognize the problem because it is measuring awareness (aided and unaided) and day-after recall, which tell you only whether the commercial broke through the surrounding media clutter—not whether the product contract is meaningful to the customer.

The point is not that creativity is without value. In a few special cases, entertainment can build a brand through imagery. The problem is that this approach requires a huge investment that most companies cannot afford. The companies that have done this successfully have been advertising their brands for years—often for decades—and have staffs of people spending millions of dollars on research to make sure that everything in the advertising builds on the carefully built image with integrity. Coca-Cola can afford to advertise this way; so can McDonalds, Budweiser, and a few others. But it's a very expensive way of doing business.

By contrast, consider a more "normal sized" company like Tropicana. It spends much less on advertising, and it focuses on relevancy—freshness, good health. Every point of customer contact deals with the benefits of drinking Tropicana's products. The package talks to health. The product is constantly expanding the healthy theme. The company's Web site is rudimentary but very effective. It talks about healthy living. The brand has huge relevancy to people because every single component, including the advertising, is focused on how drinking Tropicana's products can help you stay healthy. It is becoming synonymous with a value and lifestyle that is growing in importance. This is the kind of discipline that the vast majority of companies need to follow.

So you see, it can be done. If you take apart a Mercedes and a Hyundai and stack all the pieces in two piles (omitting nameplates and logos), chances are that most people couldn't tell the two piles apart. Put the cars back together and ride in one, even blindfolded, for a few miles, however, and you can tell which is which.

The marketing promise in the ad campaign must be delivered by the product or service. The contract must be fulfilled.

The Blight of Impatience

Because Madison Avenue can't prove that great advertising builds brands consistently, the product management system that dominates the structure of most consumer companies puts a lot of pressure on individual brand managers to find other ways to contribute to brand value in a short time. Of course, the concept of brand management is itself obsolete, so it doesn't help to keep the brand managers from abusing the very products they are paid to protect. Brand management has evolved into a race to the top of a narrow corporate pyramid: product manager to senior product manager to marketing manager to senior marketing manager to vice president of marketing to senior vice president to chief marketing officer.

This pyramid drives the industry. Instead of coming into the job with the mission of leaving the brand stronger, young marketers come in with the intention of using the brand as a springboard to move up the organization faster than their peers. The definition of how you move up depends on the organization, but it's generally based on sales figures. Remember, however, we live in an era when the average CEO in America has less than 2 years' tenure.

All of this puts a premium on quick hits to the sales line. And it didn't take brand managers long to realize that advertising, especially when it is largely irrelevant, takes a long time to pay out—it can't be built overnight, just as a brand can't be built overnight. Because people in marketing view advertising as an expense, not an investment, they want to be able to write it off and see results in the same quarter, but this is not how advertising works.

Sales Promotion: A Game of Diminishing Returns

In response to this growing trend, 15 to 20 years ago, product managers turned to sales promotion for the short-term fix they weren't getting from advertising. Sales promotion does work in the short-term. It artificially inflates the "sugar count." By dropping your customer acquisition cost with coupons or by otherwise sweetening the deal for your customers, you do generate more sales. However, rather than adding value to the brand, you are subsidizing the purchase price. This makes buying the product cheaper and increases sales—but only in the short run. Time and time again I have seen sales and market share fall back to or even below the benchmark shares once the promotional period is finished.

What's worse, it's as addictive as heroin. When the promotion ends and sales drop back down to their normal level, the pressure to mount a new promotion is almost unbearable. Furthermore, customers become trained to *expect* promotions and not to buy until a promotion is on. They become addicted to discounted prices. It's a terribly unhealthy syndrome for all involved.

This has happened in virtually every business arena—in consumer goods, in packaged goods, in retailing, in e-tailing, in business-to-business (B2B), and in business-to-customer (B2C) marketing. The problem is particularly virulent in packaged goods, where the percentage of sales at promotional prices rather than regular prices keeps growing.

The pressure on reducing retail prices comes from several directions. Retailers need to drive customers through their doors, just as e-tailers have to drive "eyeballs." They feature leading brands at lower prices as a means to this end, hoping for a "mixed" shopping cart of both regular-price and discounted products. Furthermore, store labels, which today account for 35 to 40 percent of some categories, keep the perceived price value of the branded product low.

Of course, Mom has figured it all out! To understand just how good she is at cherry picking the specials, take a close look at the weekend paper next week and show me which major retailers are driving traffic with branding versus sale events. The answer will be zero.

I have consulted in retail marketing and packaged goods for many years now. Brand advertising is great. If sales soften, however, brand advertising is the first thing to go. And it is replaced by the latest sales event at subsidized prices.

This reliance on artificial stimulants called *sales promotions* doesn't help to build long-term brand value. For example, some Internet service providers (ISPs) subsidized computer hardware prices by giving away machines (or selling them very cheaply) to people who sign up for an Internet connection. Many of these are now out of business. Something similar happened in the long-distance telephone business, where the telecom companies subsidized the cost of handsets in exchange for long-term contracts on phone service.

Don't be confused. Subsidizing the cost of product acquisition through promotions is *not* like the old razor-blade concept—sell razors cheaply so that you can make money selling the blades for years to come. There's a crucial difference in that case—the blades aren't substitutable. If you own a Gilette razor, you have to buy Gilette blades. In the case of Internet service or long-distance service, however, you can switch at will. Both have become commodity businesses, vulnerable to the latest competitive price promotion. Churn rates are sky high, and profits are scarce. The only long-term results of the rash of promotions affecting technology are that most players have gone out of business and the value of the category is cheapened in the minds of customers.

Consequently, long-distance companies and ISPs are incurring enormous customer acquisition costs, often averaging $350 to $400 per customer—yet they'll be lucky to keep these customers long enough to break even on them. They're boosting their top lines temporarily while their bottom lines continue to shrink—permanently.

During the heyday of the New Economy, the stock market supported this unrealistic business model. This has now changed. The market is finally starting to demand a healthy bottom line. It's part of the transition from the New Economy to the Next Economy, where the focus will be on maintaining a long-term relationship with customers, not one that lasts just a few months.

Thus the sales increases produced by promotions are bubble-like both in the speed at which they grow and in their fragility. Promotion-induced sales disappear quickly, and everybody gets their turn at the trough. You put your stuff on sale this weekend, and you get a boost in sales but without real profitability. Next weekend, it's your competitor's turn to do the same while you're sucking air. The result is a negative marketing cycle. At end of a year, your market share hasn't improved, and your profits have shrunk to the vanishing point.

THE FOURTH P: PRICE

Price versus Value

Let's go back to that brand value equation once again:

$$\text{Brand value} = \frac{\text{equity}}{\text{Price}} = \frac{\text{Place, Product, Promotion}}{\text{Price}}$$

There are two ways to increase brand value. If we put some numbers to the equation, the first way to increase brand value is by differentiating the brand using one or a combination of the three P's—Product, Place, or Promotion.

$$2 = \frac{20}{10}$$

You can double the value of the brand to the customer by adding equity and becoming relevant to his or her life:

$$4 = \frac{40}{10}$$

A Tropicana branding strategy would do something like this. Because most brands have not been differentiated, however, the second way of increasing brand value has become much more prevalent:

$$4 = \frac{20}{5}$$

Here, we again doubled the value of the brand, but we did so by dropping its price to the customer. In this second case, all the increase in brand value came from lowering its cost of acquisition. Hence the huge failure of marketing in the Old Economy and the New Economy. *Price is what something costs; value is what it's worth.* By focusing on price instead of value, the marketing community failed to build customer loyalty, encouraged short-list alternative-brand shopping, and made substitute shopping a reality.

Price in a World of Oligopolies

Most people believe that in a free-market economy, the traditional rules concerning price and demand are valid. According to these rules, the higher the price, the smaller is the quantity of product you'll sell. It's a simple, linear relationship.

In broad strokes, this is largely true. For example, when you combine all the products in a given category, it's usually the case that the lower-priced products will enjoy greater sales volumes than the higher-priced ones. In practical terms, however, the linear relationship between price and demand rarely works neatly for any specific product. Why is this true?

One reason is that the traditional rule assumes a completely open and frictionless marketplace with a theoretically limitless supply of competing brands. In real life, when people actually purchase a product, they are almost always operating within an oligopoly rather than in a truly free market. (As you may recall from your college economics class, an oligopoly exists whenever a market is dominated by a small number of competitors—say, three, four, or five.) Thus, for example, there might be 20 to 30 brands of toilet paper manufactured in the United States (and more than this if international manufacturers are considered), but a typical suburban supermarket might carry only 3 or 4 of these brands. There may be only 2 or 3 gas stations in your town and only 4 or 5 brands of cheese on the shelf in your local deli.

The reality, then, is that only a few sellers dominate most markets at the transaction point. And economists recognize that in an oligopoly there's generally a kinked demand curve. This means that rather than a straight line, there's a sudden cliff halfway down the line. In other words, beyond a certain point, no matter how much you lower your price, the quantity of product you'll sell doesn't increase. Why is this so?

The reason is that in an oligopoly the cost of losing market share is too great for any of the leading players to absorb. After all, if you produce and sell one of the four biggest brands of toilet paper (for example), you have a huge manufacturing, sales, marketing, and distribution machine to maintain and feed. As a result, your breakeven sales volume is very high; you can't afford to suffer a sudden huge drop in volume. Thus any price decrease by one of your competitors will trigger a matching price decrease from the others in order to avoid losing market share.

Thus, in an oligopoly, the traditional price-volume relationship eventually stops working. This explains the way most markets now work. Think about the shopping you do, whether it's for laundry detergent, CDs, or prewashed jeans. Do you choose among 20 or 30 brands or among 3 or 4? Almost certainly the latter. And while this week brand A may have a price advantage, next week it will be brand B, and the week after that brand C. By the end of the year, every major competitor has had its turn—and the market shares are remarkably stable.

Because most consumption points are oligopolistic, there are, in practical terms, only two or three price points. All products in a category are promoted at about the same price level (at different times of the year) because nobody can afford to let anyone else get markedly ahead. Since price doesn't really drive branded share, we can see that price—the fourth P—has likewise become impotent. Short-term volume increases from temporary reduced prices (TRPs) are offset by competitive TRPs in the next period. Thus, over a full year, price doesn't affect market share—only profitability.

This oligopolistic situation has existed for quite a while in most markets, but most people in marketing refuse to understand its implications. At one time, there seemed to be a clear price-quality relationship that consumers could fall back on to guide purchasing decisions. "You get what you pay for," as our parents used to say. A generation ago, this was pretty good advice. At that time, oligopolies ruled fewer markets than they do now. Technology has made it easier to duplicate competing products, reducing the differences among brands and making size matter far more than any elusive quality claim. Since you no longer get what you pay for, you might as well look for whichever product is (temporarily) priced lowest and simply buy it.

Not so long ago, the lowest-price guarantee was an important differentiating statement by a retailer. For all practical purposes, everyone offers this guarantee now. As a result, everyone is basically at the same price level. Thus, even if your favorite brand isn't on sale this week at your favorite retailer, you'll still get the lowest price—just bring in the competitive ad.

Price will be a major issue in the Next Economy, but how we manage it will be very different—and of necessity more effective. Unless the higher-priced retailers offer real brand equity, they'll go out of business. Price elasticity is not as great as economic theory suggests but rather depends on the brand equity you're dealing with. You can buy a highly trusted brand like Sony from a schlocky retailer, and you'll be happy. Eventually, the schlocky retailer's competitors will either have to match the same low price or add value to the offer to make up the difference.

THE PRICE OF FAILURE

The failure of the Four P's of marketing to protect and preserve marketing has been devastating. As the business group responsible for the customer relationship, the inability of marketers to reinvent themselves has cost their companies billions.

As we've seen, the Four P's are impotent. The concept of marketing as managing the flow of goods and services from manufacturer to consumer is false. The discipline is dead. In the Next Economy, we will need to define new applications and redefine responsibilities, for, as we'll see, in the Next Economy the customer is queen, and best-customer marketing will be the only salvation of corporate profitability.

5

The Birth of the Next Economy

If my forecast is correct, the Next Economy will arrive by 2006 and last until about 2020. Its impact will begin to be felt shortly as we approach midpoint in the decade of the naughts, for by that time the retraction from baby boomers buying products and services we now count on to fuel gross domestic product (GDP) will be felt significantly. From 2006 to 2020, we will undergo the transition from a sellers' market to a buyers' market and in the process change forever the role of marketing within the corporation.

It is difficult to overstate the impact this huge generational shift will have on business and the economy. The challenges marketers can expect in the "decade of solitude" are largely a result of this inexorable demographic pressure. This chapter will consider some of the implications.

RETREAT FROM THE MARKETPLACE

First and most significant, we can expect the baby boomers to retreat from the marketplace, just as older people traditionally have done—but in such huge numbers that the economic and social effects will be enormous. In Figure 5-1 you can see the impact that the baby boomers will have on GDP by looking at the size of the group relative to its parents.

And as the GI and depression segments age further, the baby boomers' ability to affect consumption magnifies not simply because of their size but also because of their impact on the demographics of both the war babies and gen-X generations.

Some are claiming that the baby boomers, unlike previous generations, won't make the traditional withdrawal from the marketplace. They claim that baby boomers will push retirement back or take part-time jobs. These people believe that the baby-boomer penchant for doing exactly the opposite of what history expects will result in a surging, strong economic boom into the foreseeable future. The boomers will try, but with household savings running at a *negative* rate in the United States, there's nothing left in the kitty. Millions of people are already living from paycheck to paycheck, and personal debt is at an all-time high.

The savings rate has gone from an acceptable 8.7 percent of disposable income to nothing in less than 10 years (Figure 5-2).

At the same time, personal credit has exploded (Figure 5-3).

Obviously, as these converse trends continue, the slack is taken out of the household budget. Families begin living paycheck to paycheck. The stock market becomes the equivalent of the savings plan—but with none of the security behind it.

You can see how tenuous the whole thing really is and how very important consumer confidence becomes in making sure this house of cards stays up. By 2006, it will all begin to unravel.

Figure 5-1 Relative size of key consumer generations.

Generation	Years Born	Age in 2000	U.S. Population (MM)	% U.S. Population
GI	Pre-1930	71+	25.3	9.1
Depression	1930–1939	61–70	17.8	6.5
War Babies	1940–1945	55–60	15.6	5.7
Baby Boomers	1946–1964	36–54	**77.4**	**28.2**
Gen X	1965–1976	24–35	44.9	16.4
Gen Y	1977–1994	6–23	70.7	25.8
Millennials	1995 and later	0–5	22.9	8.3

Source: Alison Stein Wellner, "Generational Divide," *American Demographics*, October 2000. Reprinted by permission.

Figure 5-2 U.S. consumer savings rate.

Year	Savings Rate, %
1992	8.7
1993	7.1
1994	6.1
1995	5.5
1996	4.8
1997	4.2
1998	4.2
1999	2.1
2000	−.1

Source: Bureau of Economic Analysis, U.S. Department of Commerce, Washington, June 29, 2001.

Figure 5-3 Annual growth in U.S. personal credit.

Year	Annual Growth, %
1996	7.9
1997	4.4
1998	5.4
1999	7.1
2000	9.5
2001	10.5

Source: "Consumer Credit," Federal Reserve Statistical Release, April, 2001.

Thus mounting evidence suggests that the baby boomers will enter their sixties psychologically and economically exhausted and ready for retreat.

The math is inescapable. Think of it this way: The average household today has about $100 per day available to spend after taxes (a bit less than $40,000 per year). Of this $100, a greater and greater percentage is going toward the first, inflationary group of items. Inevitably, there's less and less for all the other items, including those goods and services which retailers, packaged goods makers, and other manufacturers have built their businesses around. Thus the withdrawal of the baby boomers from the marketplace in which our economy gets its fuel is bound to happen.

As the baby boomers approach retirement, the situation will not improve. The average retiree needs about 65 percent of his or her final preretirement income to retire comfortably. The average 401k retirement plan, however, has a total of $35,000 in it—enough to finance perhaps 12 months of retirement. Making matters worse, only about one-quarter of those eligible to do so have opened a tax-deferred individual retirement account (IRA), and of those who have, only about 5 percent contribute regularly the maximum dollar amount permitted by law.

Some boomers will try to continue working past the age of 65. But weaker demand and lower employment levels will conspire to force most boomers out of the job market. Members of Generation Y—a group almost as large as the boomers—will take the available jobs instead. As a result, the boomers will be forced to pull back sharply on spending. It'll be less and less a question of *what* to buy and more a question of *whether* to buy.

Some have claimed that the baby boomers will be largely rescued from this financial dilemma by the wealth they'll inherit from their parents. It's true that a large intergenerational transfer of wealth is under way from the parents of the baby boomers to the baby boomers themselves. However, much of this wealth is in the form of real estate—the family homes that were bought for $18,000 in 1946 and are now worth $400,000. A house is not the same as a retirement plan. Unlike stocks, bonds, or a bank account, it generates no interest or dividends; in fact, maintaining a house costs money rather than generating it. And if the baby boomers decide to sell those houses *en masse* to help finance their retirements, it seems clear that the prices will be depressed dramatically by the appearance of a glut of houses on the market, all vying for dollars from a relatively smaller and less affluent group of potential buyers (the later generations). Thus I don't believe that the baby boomers' inheritance will be enough to restart the economy.

THE RIPPLES SPREAD

There are a number of important corollaries to the impending withdrawal of the baby boomers from the consumer marketplace—ripples spreading in widening circles throughout the entire economy.

- Goodbye intermediary. The distribution systems for products and services will become increasingly direct. Traditional intermediaries, representing the sellers in the consumption model, will be wiped out. As we'll see, these will be replaced by a new breed of intermediary representing the buyers. The Next Economy will be reborn on this swing to a buyer-side economy.
- *Money flows to Wall Street.* Investing will become an even greater obsession for tens of millions of people—removing more billions from the consumer goods marketplace. Over half of American households are invested in the equity market. We've already seen that people are reluctant to cash in stock in order to finance personal lifestyles. Every indication, including negative savings rates and explosive personal credit, is that they will begin to curb spending as their credit maxes out rather than pull out of their equity positions in the marketplace.
- *Credit cards max out.* The liquidity available to finance consumption will shrink dramatically. The number of credit cards per capita has increased over the past 4 years. We're already postponing purchases of acquired durable goods with the "Don't pay until" programs. It's hard to see how liquidity will become available when we're carrying credit card debt at 10 to 18 percent when the Federal Reserve's Fed funds rate is below 3 percent. And the amounts are huge. According to Carddata.com., the top four branded credit cards have five cards per household in circulation, with a total of $1.2 trillion in activity. How much higher can these figures possibly go?
- *Shopping: The thrill is gone.* The baby boomers will focus increasingly on lifestyle quality rather than quantity—on the security of their incomes rather than on the number of their possessions. That old fear of outliving your money becomes a reality as baby boomers head toward 60. And they're getting closer every day. The downsizing of the household and the corresponding softening of demand cannot help but be felt. Think about how much of the 67 percent of the economy is driven by the 25- to 49-year-old head-of-household segment. Think about your local mall or downtown shopping experience or your favorite Web site. Chances are the products and services offered to Mom are those she needs in her everyday management of the household. As the number of empty-nester households begins to grow exponentially,

the product and service mix requirements change significantly. Thus both the strength of demand and the consumption mix get altered at the same time by the same population bubble that altered the 1960s, 1970s, 1980s, and 1990s.

- *Boom in long-term care.* The Health Insurance Association of America says that over 40 percent of all people over age 65 will spend time in some type of nursing home. The average annual cost of such stays could reach $200,000. This realization puts some serious braking on the engines of consumer spending. If you listen closely, you can hear the sounds of those brakes quietly and slowly being applied today.

Think of it this way: Most businesses have had to make major adjustments over the past decade to survive in a + 5 percent spending environment (i.e., a world in which year-over-year spending is growing by just 5 percent). How will we deal with the coming − 5 percent environment? The impact may be devastating.

Most business sectors are becoming deflationary as a result of their success in driving costs down and the accelerating pace of innovation. A new car depreciates by 30 percent the instant its wheels hit the road, fashion keeps its value for one season at best, and no single product in a "brown goods" retailer (i.e., TV, audio, stereo, cameras) will be sold in the same form 5 years from now. In a world where all products are being redefined faster and faster, value is a rapidly wasting asset. When DVD emerges as the hot new format, the value of VHS players collapses; when everyone wants the new digital cameras, yesterday's state-of-the-art 35-mm camera is suddenly relegated to the bargain rack.

This is a taste of the upheaval awaiting business in the "decade of solitude." How will marketers cope?

HUMANIZING TECHNOLOGY

Among other things, the next 10 years will be about harnessing technology and making it work for individuals, satisfying and delighting them as customers deserve to be. The Next Economy finally will bring the long-awaited convergence of TV and the computer, and it will do so in the context of simple, life-enhancing activities. For example, a light, portable, inexpensive network appliance for e-mail will become available, an easy-to-use device that will help people do something they really want to do. And it will be as sturdy and practical as the traditional landline phone everyone owned in the 1960s—remember?—something tough enough so that it still works even if you drop it. That's the kind of technology baby boomers grew up with, and we'll go back to it eagerly.

Consider cars. The baby boomers were the first generation of Americans to embrace high-quality, low-cost foreign cars. They got used to buying and driving Hondas, Toyotas, and Nissans that used very little gas and never seemed to break down. The results:

- Booming sales of those great little cars
- Development of several powerful brands that customers really appreciated, even loved
- Willingness of baby boomers to spend anywhere from $25,000 to $80,000 on a new car—and feel great about it.

In the Next Economy, the digital technologies of the last 10 years will be reimagined along the same lines. *The technology will finally adapt to us rather than vice versa.*

The Next Economy will dismantle the foolishness of the New Economy in other ways, too. For example, the separation of clicks from bricks (i.e., digital from traditional business operations) in different business divisions will disappear. Companies such as Toys R Us, Barnes & Noble, and Macy's will realize that they have to present one face for their brand to the customer.

Does this seem obvious? Maybe it should. But until recently, New Economy enthusiasts were spinning elaborate rationales for keeping digital and traditional business operations separate. The truth is that for virtually all businesses, there is one customer, and that customer wants to be connected seamlessly with one brand.

We keep talking about brand relationships, but unless all points of customer contact are seamless and mutually reinforcing, we are presenting different promises and eliciting different expectations and responses. It's hard to have a relationship with a person suffering from multiple-personality disorder.

THE REVENGE OF THE BABY BOOMERS

The baby boomers, having been ignored and disrespected by the temporarily high-riding geeks of gen-X, will reassert their economic power over the next decade. It is under their auspices that the Next Economy will make its appearance on the stage. Here are some of the challenges we in business can expect to face as a result:

- *Services rule the roost.* The economic shift from selling products to selling services will continue and accelerate. As the baby boomers get older, they will increasingly look for services to help them enjoy a continued high quality of life. Even businesses that view themselves primarily as sellers of products will find that they have to enhance their products with related services if they hope to succeed in the next economy.
- *Customer relationships are key.* In the Next Economy, the brand experience must go beyond the transaction and consumption of the product. Every aspect of the customer's relationship with the brand will be important and must be managed properly if business hopes to keep the customer coming back for more.
- *Delighting the customer.* Businesses that succeed in the Next Economy will be those which focus not simply on satisfying customers but rather on *delighting them.*
- *Best-customer marketing.* Finally, since few businesses can afford to provide every customer with the level of service needed to delight her, most companies will find that they need to identify and focus on their *best* customers if they hope to survive and thrive in the Next Economy.

The Next Economy will be fueled by a new definition of marketing, a new set of priorities and a new skill set. Marketing became responsible for profitably building brand equity by enhancing the relationship between the brand and its customers at every point of contact. Each of these marketing touchstones will reinforce the brand relevance to its customers, thereby increasing brand loyalty. The focus of enterprise in the Next Economy will move from *what's for sale* to *why they buy.* In this buyers' economy, new, more meaningful relationships will evolve between best customers and their favorite brands.

In the rest of this book I will explore the meaning of these ideas more fully and provide some detailed and practical explanations of what your company must do to take advantage of them in the years to come.

Where Your
Customers Will Be

6

Want Segmentation

BEYOND DEMOGRAPHICS

The purpose of marketing in the Next Economy will be to understand and enhance the relationship between the brand and the customers. One of the interesting developments during the New Economy was the growth of customer relationship marketing (CRM). When banner strategy failed the business-to-customer (B2C) marketplace, marketers turned to brand advertising. Because they did not understand the differences between a label and a brand, this too failed. And so they discovered CRM.

The New Economy was, of course, driven by information. On the Internet, "cookies" left ample evidence of where people went. And detailed sales data told marketers what they bought. Yet, despite a lot of noise about how CRM would change the profitability paradigm for the dotcom community, it failed to drive business fast enough to save the New Economy companies.

The Next Economy is all about turning this *information* into *knowledge*. In the coming decade, astute marketers will be forced to delight customers by becoming proactive marketers—by anticipating their best customers' wants, using technology to simplify consumption, and representing the customer within the enterprise. What began as CRM in the New Economy will evolve into a much more intimate relationship between brands and best customers that will be capable of building profitable brand loyalty.

In the Next Economy, we marketers can't just understand *what* customers are buying; we also must understand *why* they're buying it. And we can't get there using the traditional tool for analyzing customers— that is, demographics. Demographics is an accounting model, not a marketing model. Instead, another approach is needed, one that more accurately and meaningfully captures how and why customers make the buying decisions they do.

I know, I know, want segmentation has been around since the 1960s. It's called *psychographics*, and it has been attacked viciously by the marketing establishment as being unusable, inaccurate, and (to be blunt) a lot of bull.

Not so. Anyone who's studied Maslow's hierarchy of needs remembers that once the physical concerns of an individual have been met, the motivation turns to psychological wants. We know that in most Western civilizations, commerce and gross domestic product (GDP) are driven by Mom. In this context, we have been erroneously targeting Mom's needs for over 40 years. Mom's buying what she wants, not what she needs. Her needs are quite basic and represent a small portion of her consumption, as we'll see shortly.

Demographics is based on physiology. It assumes that your age, income, and where you live have everything to do with why you buy. As a result, demographically designed marketing targets describe a seemingly homogeneous, rubber-stamp world. In a demographic world, the ideal customer family consists of

- Two adults aged 18 to 54
- With a household income over $50,000
- Living in a large urban center
- With two children living at home
- And three-quarters of a dog

One problem with this model is that this description has fundamentally nothing to do with why a family might buy the things they do. Does anyone seriously believe that any Mom ever says, "Well, I'm a married woman aged 18 to 54—I guess I'd better go to the mall this Saturday and buy 2.3 pairs of shoes"? Of course not.

Obviously, there are millions of families that fit the demographic description. But no two are really very much alike.

Tom and Karen Hennessey qualify. They're 42-year-olds living in Chicago. Tom's an accountant, and Karen is a financial planner. Their teenage kids, Beth and Lizzie, are on track for Ivy League colleges. The Hennesseys drive a Lexus, vacation in St. John's, and play golf on the weekends.

But Brian and Leah Zukofsky also qualify. They're 26-year-old performance artists living in a reclaimed factory loft on the borders of Soho in New York. Their kids, Allegra and Keno, attend an alternative nursery school. No one in the family knows how to drive. They all dress in black, have spiked hair, and attend Bjork concerts on the weekends.

And George and Helen Holmes also qualify. They're 51-year-olds who own and run a lumber yard in Dallas, which they inherited from Helen's dad, who founded the firm. Their 10- and 12-year-olds, Matt and Laura, are into soccer, horseback riding, and rock climbing. The Holmses drive an SUV and spent their last vacation touring Yellowstone.

Are you going to market your products or services to these three couples using the same appeal, the same media, the same value proposition? Good luck. And once you add to the mix their counterparts in other countries and regions of the world, the oversimplification becomes even more apparent.

Thus, having categorized millions of customers according to demographic markers—age, income, place of residence—you've gained basically *no* information about why they buy—which is the critical piece of information a marketer really needs to focus on in the Next Economy.

NEEDS VERSUS WANTS

Another problem with demographic targeting lies in the fact that it interprets customers and their buying behavior in terms of needs rather than wants. Needs satisfy the very basics of consumption. By definition, needs will always have price as the primary discriminator. Needs don't delight people—they merely satisfy them.

People need to drink ... but they want Evian.
They need clothes ... but they want Liz.

They need a car ... but they want a Porsche.
They need to get away ... but they want to go to Vegas.
They need to cut the grass ... but they want to do it on a Deere.

Don't make the mistake of assuming that average consumers are focused on fulfilling needs and that only an elite set of customers is want-oriented. This may have been true in the 1950s, in a far less affluent world where demand exceeded supply. Today, the vast majority of people and the vast majority of purchases are want-oriented.

There are many reasons for this. Of course, the enormously increased affluence of the United States and of much of the rest of the world is an important factor. So is the fact that credit is available to almost everyone in one form or another. And the broad, deep reach of modern communications technologies has further obsoleted the traditional white-collar/blue-collar divisions.

If you were to drive down the streets of middle-class America and then make the same tour of the top 25 percent of the population, you'd find more similarities than differences in what you saw. Cars, clothing, services, and much of what is in the cupboards of America are often the same brands—maybe different models, but the same brands. And with each passing year, the same reality is emerging in Europe, Japan, and the burgeoning middle-class sectors of Latin America, Asia, and the rest of the world as well.

Increasingly, consumption is aspirational, not functional. It's driven by wants, not needs. Even those without the traditional means to support the lifestyle brands they choose find ways to finance the good life. This is why personal debt is at an all-time high and savings at a record low.

In terms of consumer tastes and interests, America today is much less geographically divided than it once was. And the same can be said of the world. People everywhere are aware of the same brand names, the same fashion looks, the same fads in music and movies, and the same cars and computers and video games. Thus the old theories about market segmentation by income or geography no longer make much sense.

Here's a startling illustration. Unilever recently expanded its distribution efforts into the poorer regions of India. The company's own marketing managers believed they were likely to fail; after all, cheaper products were readily available in the local markets. Instead, they found a huge number of people willing to pay premium prices for products they perceived as the "real thing." Thus, wants can drive purchases even in financially challenged households.

People do buy to satisfy both needs and wants. In fact, during the day there are really only two kinds of things you do—things you have to do and things you want to do. (A balanced life probably includes both every day.) There are some areas of life in which a particular consumer may feel no pressing wants. A person who doesn't think much about his or her personal style may not care what wristwatch he or she wears, so he or she may buy one that simply meets the need for an accurate timepiece. It probably costs $10. On the streets of New York, you can get it for $5. Or you can spring for a Rolex at $5000. They both tell time.

This suggests one of the harsh realities of the Next Economy: *There's no margin in needs.* When people buy to satisfy needs alone, they look for the lowest price—period. It's an acquisition, not a purchase. The real profit margin comes from satisfying people's wants, not supplying their needs. There's profit in selling someone a $3500 high-definition home-theater television, not in selling them a 19-inch TV set.

Needs have value to customers only if they're handled in an efficient manner, taking as little time, money, and energy as possible. Thus, if you're in the needs business, you have to be the quickest, easiest, cheapest, or most convenient. Otherwise, get out.

A more profitable option is to segment out your best customers and give them the satisfaction of owning something special. Raise your product or service from fulfilling needs to fulfilling wants.

A bank, for example, could have a basic level of business that emphasizes speed, cheapness, and basic services while it simultaneously gets into private banking and financial counseling. Customers who qualify for the bank's want-based programs would be given a private pin number with special Internet access, a preferred initial public offerings (IPO) list, a private newsletter, international capabilities, an 800 number with access to their own personal counselor, research reports, and so on.

In this scenario, the acquisition cost of a want-based customer can be much higher than that of a need-based customer. However, the economics of converting basic services to a stepped-up want program are far more attractive because the margins are so much better. This conversion won't be based on any demographic correlation. It will be based on the customers' psychographic profile, their lifestyle priorities, their attitudes, and their behavior patterns. Furthermore, this is not solely a tool for the B2C segment of the marketplace. In the enterprise arena, knowing your customer better than your competition is a surefire way to build a loyal, long-term relationship. Any great salesperson will tell you this. If want segmentation gives you more knowledge about the hopes and aspirations of the vice president of purchasing, don't you believe you'll do a better job of selling?

Which would you rather have in your quiver—the fact that the vice president of purchasing is 45 and has two children or the fact she is 45, has two children, attends the local Baptist church every Sunday, volunteers twice a week at the children's hospital, sponsors a child in Africa, is offended by foul language on television, and believes that the school system has failed America? Would knowing more about her attitudes toward life make your sales presentation more focused? Would it be more effective? You bet it would! Just ask the top salespeople in any business-to-business (B2B) segment, and they will attest to the fact the better you know your customer, the more effective you can be at servicing her.

HOW WANT SEGMENTATION HELPS

To move the perception of your product or service from one that satisfies needs to one that satisfies wants requires brand equity—a reason to buy that goes beyond the basics of what the category offers. And you can't get there if your reach, your targeting, and your marketing are based on demographics. To move your product from water to Evian, from a car to a Porsche, from a lawnmower to a Deere, you need a relationship with the customer—and a relationship can be built only on brand equity that satisfies wants.

To understand wants and to market products and services so as to appeal to people's wants, we need to shift from demographic segmentation to *want segmentation*. Also known as *psychographics*, want segmentation is a different and much more powerful way of analyzing and interpreting today's marketplace.

Want segmentation is not a totally new method. It started because in the 1960s people's buying behaviors began to undergo a fundamental shift. Household evolution previously had been a critical part of marketing. In previous generations, when you started a family and became a full-fledged consumer, you generally emulated your parents. The patterns of buying, therefore, were reasonably predictable; marketers could chart on a graph the kinds of cars, clothes, vacations, and houses people would buy at age 30, at age 45, at age 60. In the 1960s, this began to change. People stopped emulating their parents, causing a sudden disconnect between behavior and demographics. As a result, the population could no longer be segmented accurately by demographics.

Want segmentation emerged in response to this shift. As a marketing philosophy and a practical system, it has been around for 25 years. However, it has never caught on as the dominant method of segmenting the market.

One reason: Despite the gradual decline in effectiveness of the old segmentation modeling, enough demand was generated in a growing economy to satisfy many clients. As a result, most didn't want to make the conceptual leap to a new way of thinking about customers.

Another reason: The bureaucracies of large companies—specifically their marketing and advertising departments—resisted adopting new standards and measurements in a way that's typical of bureaucracy. They never embraced the want-segmentation models available because it would have required them to reinvent themselves.

There was good reason for this rejection by the marketing establishment. The power base of all bureaucracies is based on information and budgets. Senior managers got where they were by understanding how to use the old information databases. These, in the area of targeting, were and still are largely demographically based. There was no incentive from establishment managers to use want segmentation, for it would jeopardize their power base as a source of information and dilute the budget. In other words, accepting want segmentation would only threaten their job security—not an appealing prospect for anyone.

Thus media buying is still done largely on demographics. Nielsen ratings are still body counts and largely demographic. And when the New Economy took its turn at reinventing marketing, it also used demographics as a measurement of its success—only this time, instead of bodies, it counted "eyeballs."

Also, some of the early psychographic models were more behavioral than attitudinal, and because they were touted as the "big solution" to marketing's increasing ineffectiveness, many proprietary models were introduced quickly and researched poorly. This, coupled with a rejection of want segmentation by the advertising and marketing community, ensured that this power tool could not be developed appropriately. And a fourth reason: We in the marketing and advertising industries have been measuring the wrong things. Specifically, we've been measuring and therefore pursuing cost efficiency as the central objective of marketing. In other words, we've been most concerned about reducing the cost of advertising per thousand exposures—getting the most "eyeballs" for the buck. By definition, this requires broadening the target group to lower the cost per thousand, despite the fact that this is totally ineffective as a marketing strategy. Sure, it gets us a lot of bodies in the mix, but it means that we're sending the same message out to the Hennesseys, the Zukofskies, and the Holmses. No wonder the effectiveness of marketing at generating sales has eroded.

Here's yet another reason for the relative neglect of want segmentation. The industry people who ought to use want-segmentation tools—that is, people doing creative work in advertising, designing packaging, and developing new products—weren't comfortable with the technology.

Once again, establishment managers have protected their power base by rejecting a new method of operating that would require them to relearn a skill that is critical to their success. In these cases of creativity, their argument was that profiling a customer and holding the creative within a narrow spectrum of work puts unnecessary restrictions on the creative process. It is true that talking heads are boring. *But if they talk about topics that are relevant to Mom, she'll listen.* And she'll remember who sponsored the commercial! In any case, creativity that is want-driven does not have to be boring. It can be wonderfully creative, involving, and unexpected as long as it bonds the customer to the brand's equity, not to the creative itself.

Take the current campaign by Aflac Insurance. Here is an intrusive, unexpected advertising execution using a duck and a sound byte that is memorable. The mechanism the company uses to gain your attention is the corporate name. The duck's utterance of "Aflack!" consistently reinforces the brand and directly associates it with supplemental insurance. This happens consistently at all points of contact: television, print, and outdoors. The duck is now an icon for the brand. It has both ingredients all great ad campaigns exhibit: focus (supplemental insurance) and power (the duck). It's great stuff!

Another example of ads that work right is the current Fidelity campaign focusing on the expertise of the company in helping customers manage their financial concerns. We see ordinary Fidelity people solving everyday financial problems that most of us have. It's done in a warm, credible, and reassuring manner. What makes it so good is the consistency of the tone and the obvious approachability of the company. Thus, in times of increasing uncertainty in financial markets, there seems to be a light of reason, confidence, and expertise. Another good example of focus (expertise) and power (we understand your problems). Another great one.

There's one more reason for the neglect of want segmentation. When it was first introduced, the concept of want segmentation failed. Certain companies tried to build proprietary systems and use their ability to segment markets with these systems as a business-building tool. There's nothing wrong with this idea in itself, but these companies failed to invest enough money in their systems and sold them before they were really ready. The same is true of certain published psychographic systems; for example, the VALS system created and marketed by SRI. The older versions of VALS were not well accepted. The current version of VALS is much stronger.

There are many want-segmentation systems available today, including those from Goldfarb, SRI (VALS), and Thompson Lightstone. There are other systems that have been developed specifically for use in Europe and other regions of the world. All these systems have become increasingly sophisticated, flexible, and user-friendly over time. Today, you can cross-tab want segments for any category measured by VALS. You can call Scarborough Research or Mediamark Research Institute (MRI) and get psychographics sorted by major market, by product category, by competition, by brand, and by use. The segmentation data are now available for media use right down to programming and call letters. There's no longer any excuse for not targeting by wants.

How does want segmentation work? It's a way of dividing the market by customer values—what's important to them and their attitudes toward life. These are the critical factors in understanding why people buy.

The difference between using want segmentation and not using it is like the difference between trying to sell a product to a total stranger and selling it to your spouse. If you had to sell something to your spouse, you'd know exactly how to do it—what time of day to approach him or her, what colors to use on the package, who would be the best spokesperson for the brand, what TV program to advertise on, what radio program he or she listens to while driving to work, what his or her favorite Web sites are, and so on. Want segmentation offers the ability to know your best customers with almost the same depth and intimacy.

There are differences among the various psychographic systems, but they also have a lot in common. Most of the systems sort consumers along a spectrum of values that ranges from "very conservative" to "very hedonistic." To place consumers into particular segments or "cells," the system typically asks 300 to 400 questions about what's important in people's lives. A separate group of product-based questions also may be used. Then the system links an individual's placement in a particular cell to his or her buying behavior, which of course is key.

Through many years of working with these models, the companies that maintain the systems have used the statistical technique of regression analysis to develop predictor models that allow them to analyze individuals with great cost efficiency. For example, it is possible to ask someone only 20 to 25 of the total set of 300 to 400 questions and use those few responses to place them in a cell with an acceptable degree of accuracy.

There's a reasonable amount of flexibility available in using the proprietary psychographic systems. Some of the systems are available to be used on a licensing basis, which allows other research companies to ask the proprietary predictor questions (thereby sorting customers into cells) and then tack on product questions specific to the interests of a particular client. For example, Scarborough uses the VALS system (along with some traditional demographic measures) and then studies purchase and media behaviors based on both.

THE VALS WANT-SEGMENTATION SYSTEM

To give you a more specific feeling for how want segmentation works, let's take a closer look at the psychographic cells used in the VALS system, created by SRI. VALS divides consumers into eight groupings. I will list them here in order from the most traditionalist and conservative to the most experimental and hedonistic. The eight cells and a few of their most salient characteristics are as follows:

Strugglers:
- Nostalgic
- Constrained
- Cautious

Believers:
- Literal
- Loyal
- Moralistic

Makers:
- Responsible
- Practical
- Self-sufficient

Strivers:
- Contemporary
- Approval seeking
- Style conscious

Fulfilled:
- Reflective
- Informed
- Content

Actualizers:
- Take-charge
- Sophisticated
- Innovative

Achievers:
- Goal-oriented
- Brand conscious
- Conventional

Experiencers:
- Trend conscious
- Impulsive
- Creative

To give you a slightly fuller sense of how VALS works, I will quote the fuller description provided by SRI for just two of the categories. First, actualizers:

Actualizers exhibit self-confidence and optimism. They share wide intellectual interests, engage in varied leisure activities, are well-informed, and lead active social lives. They are change leaders and are highly receptive to new products and technologies.

By contrast, here's what the systems says about experiencers:

Experiencers appreciate the unconventional. They are active and extroverted, and they like stimulation by the new, offbeat, and risky. Their lifestyle focuses on fashion, exercise, socializing, and sports.

Getting the idea? Of course, these categories involve gross generalizations. Undoubtedly, very few people fit perfectly into a single VALS box. But you can get a lot closer to the inner workings of a given consumer by first placing him or her into a broad category and then probing more deeply rather than lumping him or her together with millions of others with whom he or she shares nothing other than age and gender.

GEOGRAPHIC VARIATIONS

Although there are broad commonalties among consumers in many parts of the developed world, there are also geographic variations. As it happens, I do a lot of work in Canada, and therefore I'm closely attuned to the differences among consumers in the various regions of North America. These differences are subtle.

For example, anyone who has spent time in Montreal or Quebec City might assume that the French-Canadian population in Quebec would have very different attitudes toward fashion than "typical" Canadians. And they do. They are, in general, more fashion conscious and more forward looking in their tastes. This is not because all French-Canadians are born with a genetic predisposition to looking great. It is simply because the percentage of Quebecers who fall into the fashion-conscious segment is higher than anywhere else.

It takes judgment and skill to determine the best way to respond to this kind of difference. There's a whole French-speaking marketing and advertising community in Quebec that has convinced its clients to run separate, unique campaigns in the province. Their argument: "We're different—we're French. Your Anglo stuff won't work with us." But the evidence demonstrates otherwise. The same campaigns that work for other fashion-conscious consumers work just fine with the French speakers of Quebec (adapted from English into French, of course).

The fact is that the fashion-conscious shoppers of Quebec are no different from the fashion-conscious shoppers of Calgary, Alberta—or New York. They just happen to speak a different language. And as time passes, the same is becoming increasingly true about fashion-conscious shoppers in Mexico City, Dublin, and Tokyo as well.

PUTTING WANT SEGMENTATION TO WORK

Finding the right customers will be so critical in the next economy that want segmentation will become even more crucial than it already is. To begin with, the implications for advertising are enormous. Gross rating points (GRPs) will no longer matter—it'll be the quality of the people watching. In the Next Economy, media will eventually charge for advertising slots based on the quality of the audience rather than the quantity. And companies will gladly pay a premium to be in front of a larger proportion of their best customers.

Advertising can no longer rely on lowest-common-denominator creative. Instead, the creative content will have to be designed so that the best customers can relate to it. Note that psychographics does not supplant creativity or produce mindless, paint-by-numbers marketing plans. The idea is to focus creativity in a way that's relevant to people. Rather than a shotgun aimed at the widest possible audience, our advertising will be more like a rifle targeted at the real values and wants of specific people. The more our creative talents understand the people they're talking to, the better the creative work can become.

The goal is to relate to our customers as best friends. And we can't get to this level of intimacy and involvement without want segmentation. In the Next Economy, the power base will shift. People who want to become relevant to Mom will have to start by understanding what she wants from us rather than what we want from her. This requires understanding her values, her attitudes, and what she wants from life. Want segmentation makes this possible.

Once you're convinced of the value of want segmentation, what do you do with it? The first step is to find a want-segmentation model that suits your business. There are a number of good ones besides VALS. For example, here's a sampling of recently developed segmentation systems designed particularly for classifying the lifestyles and marketplace behaviors of Internet users:

Ebates.com Dot-Shoppers divides e-shoppers into six categories:
- Clicks-and-mortar
- Ebivalent newbies
- Hooked, online, and single
- Hunter-gatherers
- Time-sensitive materialists
- Brand loyalists

Pew Internet User Types identifies four kinds of Internet users:
- Newcomers
- Experimenters
- Utilitarians
- Netizens

Technographics Segments classifies consumers in 10 categories based on their attitudes toward technology:
- Fast forwards
- New Age nurturers
- Mouse potatoes
- Technostrivers
- Digital hopefuls
- Gadget grabbers
- Handshakers
- Traditionalists
- Media junkies
- Sidelined citizens

Feeling confused yet? Don't. The differences among all these systems (with their cute and catchy category names) are less profound than you might assume. If you experiment with two or more systems, you soon begin to notice large areas of overlap among the categories described. After all, there are only so many ways to think about consumers.

All the best want-segmentation models have associated behavior attached to the model. One reason I like VALS is that I can take it back into large customer databases that are already available and cross-tabulate the want-segmentation model into a myriad of products, services, banners, and labels. This enables me to tell you, for example, the market for any retailer or brand in most major categories as segmented by the VALS model: so many strugglers, so many believers, so many makers, and so on. These data are available directly from VALS, from Scarborough, and from other research companies.

Once we know the participation rates by cell for the category—and even more important, for our customers—we can begin to create marketing programs that are very empathetic to their wants. Then we can tie our advertising to a media plan that focuses not on the number of "eyeballs" we'll reach (as in the old demographic approach) but on the favorite programs, magazines, and other media that our targeted cells patronize. We'll know the best times of day to reach them and how to talk to them most empathetically.

Why buy time during NFL football when your targeted cell is a very small percentage of the football audience? You may be able to reach the same number of people from that cell for a fraction of the cost by buying VH1 or American Movie Classics on cable. It's the quality of the audience that matters, not the quantity.

The value of psychographics extends beyond advertising. Manufacturers can design and market products for different segments as well. Remember, advertising is only one of those all-important points of contact between our brand and the customers. Packaging is another. It's possible to create packaging targeted to each psychographic segment, which can be a significant driver of impulse sales.

Channels of distribution are another point of contact. People in particular cells shop at certain stores more often. Thus, once you know your target cells, you know which stores need to carry, display, and promote your product most aggressively. The actual features of the product also could be tailored to specific groups of customers.

WANT SEGMENTATION AND THE INTERNET

Right now, a company's Web site generally is designed in a one-size-fits-all way. However, the interactive capabilities of the Internet and the relatively low cost of customization suggest that this strategy is wrong for the medium. How people enter and navigate your Web site could be very different for different groups of customers. Why not create different doors to your site depending on how the Web surfer enters it? You could have one entrance to your site but then break surfers down by category depending on what he or she buys and where he or she buys it. If you know, for example, that people from one of your target cells are constantly looking for useful information (fulfilleds, for example), you might want to build them a special Web site with pin-number access that is loaded with product data, how-to tips, chat rooms where customers can exchange ideas about using the product, and so on. By contrast, another group of consumers—strivers, perhaps—is interested in image and approval. A Web site tailored to them might be filled with product endorsements from well-known celebrities and photos of the product in use in high-prestige settings.

Want segmentation has the potential to play an enormous role in realizing the business potential of the Internet. This potential lies in the ability of the Web to provide customized, personal information in a cost-effective manner. The Net is now largely a need-oriented marketing system because only price is the differentiator. People generally buy books, CDs, and travel services on the Internet because they believe bargains are to be had and because it's convenient. When the Next Economy is in full swing, they'll be buying there because they have personal accounts with their favorite vendors who have customized their offerings to suit the individual's purchase desires.

Today, the few highly effective destination Web sites are want-based—people go to them because they want to buy something that meets a personal and emotional need. So far, first-in-category pure plays (like Yahoo!, Amazon, and eBay) and the bricks-and-clicks companies—those with both an online and an offline presence, like Lands' End, L.L. Bean, Wal-Mart, K-Mart, and Macy's—are winning this battle. These companies have strong relationships with their customers, developed through years of traditional marketing—that is, the brand has equity with the customer. They use these relationships to provide customers with satisfaction of their wants. The stronger the desire, the better is the relationship between the customer and the Web site.

Want segmentation also means that in the near future the database and infrastructure people—that is, the companies that gather, track, interpret, and supply the information about the people who are on the net—will explode exponentially. They include the companies that track "cookies," such as Doubleclick; portals such as AOL, Yahoo!, and MSN; researchers, such as Forrester, Boston Group, and Jupiter; and the Internet efforts of Microsoft.

Over the course of the Next Economy, B2C business on the Internet will be transformed into a want-segmentation business. Even now, small companies with modest revenues of a million dollars a year are doing great on the Web. They have no overhead and no incremental costs at all, and they are adding volume every single year—because they're dealing in wants. There are thousands of these worldwide. Almost every hobby has multiple sites. Every want is represented, from specialty X-rated adult content sites to used-car sites. Every car brand is represented, from Porsche to Beetles. Own a dog? How about a visit to dogtoys.com? Do you happen to be into cats? Try catfurniture.com. Do you love classical guitars? Log onto lmii.com for luthiers and makers of fine guitars. Or maybe you want to buy and sell coins, antique books, or ceramic vases. All are very well represented online.

By contrast, big players like *Time* magazine can't make money on the Web because they provide information that's available elsewhere. They focus fundamentally on *what's going on*—which is a need. However, when you want to know *why*, you've shifted from need to want and into a more specialized area of knowledge. Thus, if you're a butterfly collector, a rabid rugby fan, a ski aficionado, or an antiques lover, you'd love a site dedicated to you, and you'd visit it even if it cost money.

Consider an example from the realm of financial information. TheStreet.com started out as a subscription service. It provided hot tips about trends on Wall Street, explaining *why* things happened. This follows a familiar pattern: Those who make money on financial information make money on the *why*—think of people like Dow Jones, publishers of *The Wall Street Journal* and *Barron's*, the newsletter publishers, and the high-profile financial advisors. But TheStreet.com lost patience. It stopped being a subscription service covering insights into trends and became instead a free service (supported by advertising) offering stock quotes, financial headlines, and other data on *what* was happening. As soon as it did so, it lost its market.

On the Web, *what* is a free business. It happens everywhere, every 15 minutes. *What* satisfies a need. But people will pay for *why*. *Why* satisfies a want.

There are people who believe that selling real-time quotation services by subscription is successful because it provides faster delivery of the information. I don't think so. The folks I know who subscribe to financial subscription services do so because they can only understand the bid and ask prices by seeing the live data and the changes in these data in real time. They make their money in anticipation of the next change, not on the present. They are looking for trends and anomalies. They want to know *why*, not *what*.

WANTS AND SHARED VALUES

It's hard for people to understand, but people who drive Porsches sometimes have better relationships with other Porsche drivers than with their own families. The makers of Saturn cars also created a similar sense of community. A nuclear family is usually need-based. (The closest families evolve into want-based groups.) However, an external, want-based family is built around shared values; what's relevant in their lives is relevant to one another. A meaningful club membership is like this, whether the club is a local acting group, the Porsche owners club, a club of bird watchers or ice fishers, or whatever. It is remarkable how well perfect strangers get along when they share values. If you're ice fishing and something goes wrong, another ice fisher surely will help you. If your Saturn breaks down, another Saturn driver will stop to help.

Exactly the same thing can happen with brands. They become relevant to people when they connect with shared values. Thus relevant companies that could become (in psychological terms) members of the Porsche owners club might be companies that make high-end tires or prestigious automobile accessories, companies that offer customized high-end travel packages, companies that sell stylish sportswear, and so on.

As this example illustrates, sometimes the most effective way to brand something is to become associated with a shared value. In the Next Economy, where people are withdrawing from consumption as the aging baby boomers are starting to do, the last thing people will withdraw from is their shared values. These are a source of pleasure to them. They want to stay connected. If they have to cut back on their spending, they'll eliminate first the things they don't care much about;

they'll hold onto their beloved Porsche and their flower club activities as long as they can. Thus, for the brand, becoming affiliated with a shared value is one key to your customer relationships.

HOW WANTS CHANGE

The structure of dominant wants is constantly changing because values change all the time. We call this *growing*. But it's simply a reflection of our cumulative experiences in life and our aspirations going forward. Neither of these two variables is static. Thus the science of want segmentation cannot be static either.

One dramatic example is that in the 1980s people bragged about how *much* they paid for things, whereas in the 1990s they bragged about how *little* they paid. For a company, getting caught on the wrong side of such shifts is very dangerous. Thus, for your brand's values to remain relevant, they must be constantly evolving. This is blasphemy to traditional, need-based marketers. But it's a truth that will only grow in importance in the Next Economy.

In the 1970s, you couldn't trust anybody over 30. In the naughts, you can't trust anyone *under* thirty. In the 1980s, we aspired to the 30-hour work week; in the 1990s, we loved to complain about working $7 \times 24 \times 365$. In the 1970s, we shared everything with everybody; in the 1990s, we were paranoid about privacy.

Unlike needs, which are relatively unchanging, wants can be tremendously volatile. This is the scary part of want segmentation: If you don't do your homework, you can seriously damage the brand. Although it can be dangerous to shift your brand's relevancy in pursuit of ever-moving customer values, the greater danger lies in not changing with the times.

Of course, shifting your brand's perceived equity isn't the same as completely redesigning the product. In most cases, in fact, the brand's physiology stays the same while its personality, its perceived equity, and its unique appeal get carefully modified.

Successful companies operating in the Next Economy will come to understand that Old Economy strategies that are static and rigidly defined cannot possibly work in the Next Economy. Neither can New Economy strategies that talked about speed, efficiency, and category dominance but had no strategic relevance. In this next iteration, business must build strategic vision on the basis of the relevance of the brand to their best customers. This means that shared values are critical to brand equity. And this, in turn, means that strategy must evolve into contract commitments that service and delight your best customers. Strategy in the Next Economy is customer-focused, not corporate-focused. It starts with what customers want to buy from you, not what you want to sell them. And because we are focused on people instead of products, the brand will change—gradually but perceptibly—every year.

Consider Disney and Cadillac as examples of continuity with change. Fifteen to twenty years ago, Cadillac was in big trouble, in large part because it had made its body styles interchangeable with other GM vehicles. Thus it broke its contract with their customer.

The whole point of branding, of course, is to be distinctive. Today, Cadillac is doing much better because of the North Star power plant, the OnStar technology, and the beginning of a distinctive look and feel to the product line. And while the technological details and styling change from year to year, the underlying relevance of the Cadillac brand—upscale driving luxury for the person who has "arrived" financially and socially—is finally on the mend. The contract has begun to be reestablished. Today, you can buy a Cadillac pickup, a Caddy SUV, or a traditional Cadillac sedan. *Cadillac* is beginning to mean "the best" once again. Whether it will be the best in America or the best in the world remains to be seen because the values associated with being the best are always changing.

Similarly, Disney is successful because it has evolved the definition of *imaginative family entertainment* as the wants of its target audience have evolved. If Disney had continued making the kinds of nature films and corny comedies it made in the 1960s and 1970s, it would be out of business today. Instead, Disney developed more sophisticated styles to satisfy the wants of a hipper young crowd while still maintaining the atmosphere of wholesome family fun that the baby boomers (now parents and even grandparents) grew up with decades ago.

Today, any point of contact the Disney brand has with its customer base reinforces wholesome family fun. From licensed products to movies to Disney stores to theme parks, there is consistent shared value expressed and experienced. Where potential opportunities present themselves that are not compatible with this value, Disney does not break its contract. This is why Disney created a second motion picture brand—Touchstone Pictures—for movies that don't fit under the Disney banner. Which movies end up as Disney versus Touchstone will evolve over time, but the strategy of having both segments available is sound and will carry the company well through the Next Economy.

NEEDS AND WANTS IN B2B BUSINESSES

The belief exists in some quarters that dealing with wants is a B2C concept and therefore basically irrelevant to B2B companies. This is not so. As I've said, the people who make purchasing decisions in companies are human beings, just like consumers. Therefore, they too have emotional and psychological interests and wants that ought to be fulfilled by companies that are doing business with them.

Furthermore, remember that there's no B2B if it's not followed by B2C. Over two-thirds of the GDP is driven by consumer spending. Thus, in virtually every case, a B2B transaction is just a step along the way to the ultimate consumer. The machine tools, office supplies, computer software, and other commercial products you sell to corporate customers are in service to an ultimate B2C consumer. Thus suppliers and vendors need to be cognizant of consumer needs and provide products and services that will help their customers meet those needs.

Here's a specific example. Magna supplies automobile parts to manufacturers. If a design group under contract to General Motors is working on a new car to fit a want vision, then the B2B people at Magna are involved in want segmentation whether or not they realize it. Therefore, the more they understand the want model of consumer behavior, the better they'll understand what the GM engineers must have in order to create a car that will sell and sell, and the better they can contribute to its success. Shared values at work in a B2B environment!

Or take a look at BMW automobiles. Back in the 1970s, the only "ultimate driving machine" from BMW was a 2002tii. Everything else the company made was quite pedestrian. But the company understood that moving the brand from need-driven transportation to want-oriented driving satisfaction could be a brand repositioning that generated margin and a worldwide demand for a sporty luxury automobile. In borrowing a page from Volkswagen, the boxy, cute little 2002 gave way to a larger, sporty, and stylish 3 Series that led to the 5 Series, the 7 Series, and the 6 Series. Today, BMW's success has been built on maintaining focus (sporty luxury) and power ("the ultimate driving machine").

Or look to writing instruments and watches as two other categories of product where wants and needs have separated. Those corporations working in the need segment are rewarded for low production costs, high efficiency, and ubiquitous distribution. The Bics and Timexes of the world have built a great business here. But the margins are in the want segment. Mont Blanc and Rolex are rewarded for design and stature. You can write and tell time with both ends of the spectrum. But one brand cannot be all things to all people.

GLOBAL BRANDING AND WANT SEGMENTATION

"Wait a minute," you may be thinking. "If one brand can't be all things to all people, how does *global branding* work?"

This is a good question. My short answer is: It doesn't. Or, to be more precise, global branding has so far met with only limited success.

Global branding is more a matter of organizational strategy than of marketing strategy. It's built around the desire to centralize and consolidate manufacturing and marketing in the name of increased efficiency. On the manufacturing side, it may work; the economies of scale that can be realized through massively centralized production may offset the incremental costs of shipping the product worldwide. However, production costs are usually only a tiny fraction of the marketing budget. Saving a few hundred thousand dollars isn't the real motivation for centralizing marketing. In truth, it's purely a control issue.

Today's global marketers assume that a single brand can become relevant to a broad international target market, defined by demographics. This is possible, however, only if you water down the brand's equity to its lowest common denominator. The inevitable result is that the brand loses relevancy for its best customers.

It is not possible for a lowest-common-denominator brand equity to succeed in widely differing cultures. Despite the current push to unify Europe economically, the countries of Europe are still marked by very different sets of values. And anyone who has traveled to Asia and Africa would be hard pressed to describe the common values that unite the billions of consumers living on those two continents.

Even within North America, there are subtle but significant differences in wants between the United States and Canada. We share a common language—at least, most of us do—but American values are largely shaped by the Constitution and by a Declaration of Independence that asserts the right to "life, liberty, and the pursuit of happiness." Canadian values, by contrast, were formed by the British North American Act, which guarantees law, order, and good government. The American icon is the bald eagle, a lone, sky-roving predator; the Canadian icon is the beaver, a social, lodge-building mammal. The United States was settled by homesteaders who carved individual farms out of the wilderness; Canada was settled by employees of the Hudson's Bay Company who clustered near the protective forts the company built. Americans want to stand out; Canadians want to fit in. (Hence the placatory syllable Canadians append to any assertion that might provoke disagreement: "It's a beautiful morning, *eh?*")

If two countries with so much in common, including a continent, a language, and a commitment to democracy, can have such different value structures, how can countries from Europe, Asia, Latin America, and Africa all rally around a single brand?

Nonetheless, several successful global brands *do* exist. Almost all of them are aspirational, based on the values and attitudes of a minority of people who share the same lifestyle and values as their counterparts in countries around the world. Luxury brands like Mercedes, Rolex, Polo, and Donna Karan are examples. These brands have, in effect, segmented on a want basis by appealing to a value structure that supersedes the cultural mores of individual countries.

What about Coke and Pepsi? Do they represent nonaspirational global brands? Maybe so. But the price for creating these two brands has been enormous. Coke and Pepsi throw so much marketing money at their brands that local competition simply cannot afford to fight them. Their vulnerability is suggested by the fact that in large areas of the world, both Coke and Pepsi *are cheaper than water.*

The future of global branding will depend on how relevant any given brand can be made, on a local basis, to a specific want segment of the economy. Marketers with worldwide branding responsibilities will need to invest in proprietary psychographic research to accurately divide the local cultures by wants. Only then will they be able to determine whether a global, regional, or national positioning makes sense of the brand.

In the Next Economy, increasingly the pendulum will swing from global to local marketing priorities.

LOBLAWS: A CASE STUDY IN SHIFTING FROM NEEDS TO WANTS

The grocery business remains one of the most feudal systems in business. There are little kingdoms within every supermarket chain where regional buying is duplicated all over the place. The excuse for this decentralization is that it is necessary to satisfy regional tastes. In reality, however, these are fiefdoms run on a political basis, and they pose a big barrier to success in the industry.

Nonetheless, there are huge opportunities in the grocery business for anyone who is interested in building a want business that is truly differentiated. The average family shopper buys groceries once or twice a week and blows a lot of money on them. A store that manages to tap into the want part of the equation can make this normally low-margin business far more profitable.

However, very few food companies have tried to do this. Most have focused on needs rather than wants. They are battling in the middle of the market. The private-label/store-brand business is an example. Each of the grocery chains has duplicated the look and feel of the branded leaders in each category—cheeses, soft drinks, etc. The result has been look-alike products backed by reduced marketing spending and therefore reduced prices.

Some of the chains have grabbed market share in this way. In many areas where products are basically commodities—paper products, juice, milk—some private labels are doing well, controlling some 20 to 35 percent of market. Yet the retailers still aren't making a lot of money–their margins are in the low single digits in most cases. Why? Because reduced share for the national brands means that the retailers are losing cooperative marketing and warehousing allowances, volume rebate allowances, drop shipping allowances, and other moneys paid by these brands to the retailers. Thus the retailers' business strategy cannot generate margins because they are making money on their buying, not on their selling.

Within the last 10 years, Loblaws, a chain of grocery stores in Canada owned by Weston, has developed a partial solution to this dilemma. This company did it by becoming one of the first food chains to use want segmentation, and it helped the company produce a breakthrough strategy.

The beauty of a retailer looking at wants is that its customers are always in the stores, which makes it easy to ask them what they want. Loblaws did just this, using in-store and telephone questionnaires to question customers. This led to a great strategy for distinguishing Loblaws from such major competitive banners as A&P, Miracle Food Mart, and Dominion stores.

Grocery managers recognize two parts to every food store: the perimeter and the middle. The perimeter departments represent freshness; they include produce, meat and fish, dairy, bread, and the deli counter. The middle of the store focuses on packaged goods—items in cans and boxes bearing such brand names as Kraft, Kellogg, Campbells, and so on, as well as paper goods, laundry products, and so on.

Conventional wisdom has always been that the marketing opportunity is on the perimeter, which is where most of the competitive battles have been fought. Stores work hard to differentiate themselves on the perimeter via appealing presentation, noticeable freshness, and impeccable cleanliness. While most big-brand marketing dollars come from the middle of the store, most of the profit margins have come from the perimeter.

Loblaws figured out that it could differentiate the middle as well as the perimeter by making wants part of the middle of the store—in effect, making the middle into a new strategic battle zone.

The key was realizing that store brands could go above the national brands in quality—in effect, meeting wants that the other brands were ignoring. Accordingly, Loblaw's launched the President's Choice line of high-end store-brand products. The company set quality standards for these products noticeably higher than those of the leading national-brand products. For example, President's Choice Decadent Cookies, the company claimed, contained more chocolate than any national brand.

It was a stunning and counterintuitive move. After years of vendors being told to cut costs, now the message was reversed. The downward spiral of reducing costs to save fading margins was changed—now, building differentiation into the product, although costly, became key to reviving margins.

Then, using the higher margins that the higher-priced, want-based products created, Loblaws was able to reposition the store as an adventure in food marketing, finding unique and differentiated products from around the world that people wanted and putting them on the shelves. As a result, Loblaws soon became the most profitable grocery chain in Canada, a position I believe it retains to this day.

It has been so successful that the brand has now been licensed, and non-competing food retailers can now source President's Choice product. The company has even moved the brand into financial services, where it continues to do well.

The strategy has changed how people look at grocery stores. Looking with a fresh eye, retailers are now asking what else people might want from their grocery shopping experience. The perimeter is changing, supplementing the traditional emphasis on freshness with convenience, expanding the offerings of prepared foods, and adding such services as banking, dry cleaning, travel, and package delivery. Thus supermarkets have become part of the remaking of retailing driven by want-based strategy.

THE HARLEY MYSTIQUE: BUILDING A WANT-BASED BRAND

No one *needs* to ride a Harley-Davidson motorcycle. But this is a brand that taps so powerfully into the wants of millions of people that it has evolved beyond motorcycles into accessories, clothing, travel, insurance, shipping, and a vast array of hard goods—bar stools, watches, wallets—that have nothing to do with motorcycles. In dozens of arenas, the Harley-Davidson logo is golden. How many customers have tatooed *your* company's logo on their bodies?

It wasn't always that way. The brand has been around ever since Arthur Harley and Walter Davidson pieced together their version of a single-cylinder motor bicycle in an era when motorcycles were more of a need than a want and when the new Harley-Davidson brand competed with over 300 other U.S. manufacturers. Not until June 1981, when the employees and management of Harley-Davidson bought the failing company from AMF, did its metamorphosis from product to brand begin.

I'm sure that a demographic profile for the "typical" Harley rider exists somewhere in the company's marketing vaults in Milwaukee. But I also suspect that if you attended a meeting of HOG (the Harley Owners Group) or dropped in on bike week in Laconia, Daytona, Sturgis, or

Lake George, you'd be hard pressed to find many people who resembled the demographic average.

Harley owners can't be defined demographically because they didn't buy the machine because of their age, income, or education. People buy Harleys to make a statement—to strike out against conformity. The Harley logo stands for individuality. Hog owners don't want to fit in—they want to stand out.

Fittingly, no two Harleys are the same. Sure, they come off the assembly line in cookie-cutter style with a limited number of options packages to choose from. But the customization starts at the dealer long before anyone takes possession of the bike, and it continues with a host of modifications, large and small, made by the proud owner to ensure that his or her beast is even more unique. Thus there's no real "Harley look," because no two Harleys look alike. But there is a Harley culture, built around individualism, and a Harley fraternity, made up of folks who share the same values and will go out of their way to help one another.

The Harley logo carries a cachet that permits premium pricing and healthy margins, even in categories such as clothing, fashion accessories, footwear, and housewares, where overall profits of more traditional brands have been deteriorating steadily. Harley's success has come about because of this careful nurturing of the Harley mystique. Whether you're a Wall Street broker astride a Dresser or a minimum-wage busboy riding a used 883, you're part of the Harley family. It's not about demographics—it's about shared wants, aspirations, and values.

Until Loblaws and Harley-Davidson remade their companies on the basis of wants rather than needs, it wasn't at all obvious to most observers that this was possible. Yet the leaders of those companies perceived the opportunity and seized it, leaving their competition wondering what had happened. If you're in an industry where most companies are still stuck in the trap of thinking needs rather than wants, why not be the first to break away? There are huge rewards waiting for those who do.

7

Quintile Marketing

As you may have surmised, it's a huge fallacy to believe that all customers are created equal. They're not. In the business-to-customer (B2C) space, if you could know how much revenue and profit an individual customer represented as she came through your front door or logged onto your Web site, you would treat her very differently. There are some customers you don't want if you can avoid them. They cost you an arm and leg because of the way they purchase. By contrast, others generate the bulk of your profits. In the Next Economy, the withdrawal from spending of many of the baby boomers will make it critical for you to know which is which. *Finding your best customers and focusing your business and marketing strategies on serving them will be a prerequisite for success.*

The basic definition of strategy is *focus* and *power.* The art of strategy begins with deciding what to focus on—which of the customer wants is most relevant to her and can most consistently be delivered by your brand. The second part of the art of strategy is determining how to put enough resources behind this relevant point of difference so that the customer notices it and associates it clearly with your brand.

Of course, this isn't easy to do. It can be hard to recognize which customers are truly valuable and which ones aren't. And once you've identified them, it can be hard to tailor your marketing and service programs to treat them appropriately. In fact, many businesses find it hard even to stop treating their best customers like their worst, and vice versa. This chapter should help solve the problem.

YOUR WORST AND BEST CUSTOMERS

Who, then, is your worst customer? She has a number of easy-to-recognize characteristics:

- She buys your brand only when it is on sale—never at full price.
- She returns goods frequently, incurring large service costs.
- She interacts with your brand a couple of times a year at most.
- She complains about your supposed shortcomings to everyone she can talk to.
- She sees you as nothing more than a necessity for fulfilling a need.
- She has no loyalty to you, despite your efforts at relationship-building.
- She will switch to another brand in a heartbeat, the moment she thinks she can save a dime or a dollar by doing so.

By contrast, these are the distinguishing marks of your best customer:

- She buys your brand as part of a basket of goods, including both high-margin and low-margin items.
- She buys your brand regularly, whether you're on sale or not.
- She uses your product category on a regular, ongoing basis.
- She tells friends about her experiences with you.
- She forgives you when you make a mistake.
- She knows your brand, the store where you're distributed, and some of its employees.
- She won't switch to another brand unless you force her to by abusing the relationship.

As you can imagine, the best customer is the source of most of your revenues and the vast majority of your profits. Because she buys from you consistently, the sales she generates are consistent and high-margin. And because she is willing to help you help her, she is ultimately less costly to service than your worst customer.

Clearly, if you could find, encourage, nurture, and grow your best customers, the benefits to your business would be enormous. Best-customer marketing, then, is a key to success in the Next Economy, when so many customers will be withdrawing from the marketplace. Under such circumstances, everyone's best customers will be more precious than ever.

This concept is easy to see and accept. It's a variation on the well-known 80/20 rule. The problem, of course, is turning it into a practical plan of action.

WASTED MARKETING EFFORT

Businesspeople have been chuckling ruefully for a century about the old quip by legendary retailer John Wanamaker: "I know that half of my advertising budget is wasted. The only trouble is, I don't know which half." In the world of mass communications, the quip is as true today as it was 100 years ago. Clearly, for most companies it's not an effective use of your advertising dollar to buy time or space in a mass medium such as newspapers or network television, given the fact that only a small fraction of the audience you're buying is likely to ever become a customer for your brand—let alone one of those all-important best customers. And there's resistance to targeting mass advertising more precisely. As we've discussed, this is one important reason why mass communications has become largely irrelevant to changing customer behavior today.

An alternative to which many in marketing and advertising have turned is one-to-one marketing via mail, Web site, or telephone. Unfortunately, the experience of the past 20 years suggests that this alternative usually doesn't work very effectively either. Old Economy direct-marketing results vary widely by category, but return rates of less than 1 percent are experienced in mass distribution. This makes Old Economy direct mail very expensive. In fact, the firms that promote one-to-one marketing have invented entirely new financial concepts in an attempt to justify its high cost. They came up with the notion of "lifetime value," saying that the high acquisition cost of a new customer was small when compared with the value of all the purchases that customer would make throughout her lifetime—say, over the next 20, 30, or 40 years. This reasoning is ludicrous. Most of us can't even keep our marriages together for a lifetime—so how can we assume that our tele-marketers have the power to win a customer who will keep sending you money for the rest of her life?

For the most part, direct-marketing customer-acquisition costs are simply too high to be affordable by most product categories. The assumption that direct marketers make, which is that a converted cus-tomer stays loyal throughout her life, flies in the face of the huge amount of brand switching taking place today.

As we moved from the Old Economy to the New Economy, mar-keting practitioners continued to press this lifetime-value measure-ment. The predictable results were an indication of business management's refusal to use common sense. How can you run acquisi-tion costs of $350 to $500 in a category that generates revenue of $600 per year? How can you justify this acquisition cost and its inherent life-time value when you know from your own sales numbers that the churn rate (the rate at which people leave your brand) is running at 40 to 60 percent a year? If this is the annual rate, there's not much of a lifetime to look forward to, is there?

We knew that general mass-media direct-response advertising for on-page couponing ran between two-tenths of 1 percent and 5 percent. So why did we buy the argument that banner advertising would gener-ate sales when this is the New Economy version of the same old con-cept?

When the Internet came along, the one-to-one marketers thought it might represent the breakthrough they'd all been looking for. You can e-mail thousands of potential customers at a cost of a fraction of a penny each, as compared with 50 cents or more for sending a flyer via "snail mail." Thus the cost part of the equation, it seemed, might finally be under control. Unfortunately, the sales results didn't hold up their end of the bargain (although I must admit that some recent direct-response e-mail campaigns can generate 15 to 20 percent response rates—*if* they are carefully targeted and focused on wants and values).

It is not surprising to find that what does work in direct marketing in the Old Economy will be the cornerstone of the Next Economy. This is relevancy. What separates effective marketing from junk mail is relevancy. What separates effective marketing from "spam" is relevancy. What affects response rates is relevancy. And what makes communica-tions relevant is who they are targeted toward.

The Next Economy will allow us to use both relevancy and targeting—not through mass marketing or one-to-one marketing, but through quintile management.

THE SOLUTION: QUINTILE MANAGEMENT

In the Next Economy, the challenge will be to find customers with whom we can have economically sustainable relationships. It's obvious that neither a mass-marketing strategy nor a one-to-one strategy will be the answer. The right answer is what I call *quintile management*. It is simply a segmentation strategy for identifying and focusing on your best customers while preventing your worst customers from draining away your resources.

Here's how it works. You start by taking all your customers and ranking them in order according to the number of dollars they spend with you in the course of a year. Depending on the kind of product or service you sell, you may want to factor in frequency of purchase as well so as to avoid misranking the person who spends a lot of money with you without creating a long-term relationship. For example, when I developed a quintile management program for a major North American department store, I had to be careful to adjust the dollar value of a customer by considering purchase frequency as well so that a customer who came in to buy a kitchen full of appliances but never visited the store at any other time didn't rise to the top of my list.

Perhaps you're wondering whether the data needed to rank your customers in this way are readily available. For nearly all businesses, they are or could be. Retailers, for example, can get individual customer sales figures by studying sales charged on their credit cards. If you're a direct marketer via phone, mail, or Internet, it's obvious that the information you need is available somewhere in your system. If you're in the business-to-business (B2B) universe, your sales staff probably has the data, although they may currently be in somewhat fragmented form.

Some companies, such as those which sell products mainly through third-party retailers or distributors, may find it more challenging to identify and rank their customers. These companies may have to create a program to meet the need for data. Consumer goods companies that sell semidurables and durables can rely on the warranty cards to establish current customer lists. Packaged goods companies that have a high frequency of purchase can use clubs or affinity/loyalty programs to obtain the information. The key is to do four things:

- Gather transactional data and associate them with a household that can be reached.
- Keep the list current.
- Track cumulative household sales.
- Obtain permission to get more information on the household that will help you service it more effectively.

What all these things have in common is that they require some form of registration by customers that makes it possible for you to record and track their purchases on an ongoing basis.

Obviously, you won't capture information about every one of your customers using these methods. However, you will find that if you promote your program aggressively, you will capture a reasonably high percentage of them. And by comparing how many transactions you're running with the sales recorded in your customer club database, you can get a pretty good sense of what fraction of your business you are able to identify and analyze.

Of course, the Internet can be an enormous ally in this effort. Again, some kind of affinity program will be needed to get consumers of your brand to register with you somehow. The key is to create a direct relationship with them. This isn't hard to do if the product or service you sell is a high-ticket, complex, or highly involving item—high-end home theater components, for example, or rare sports memorabilia. It's harder when you sell products or services that are inexpensive or commodity-like. The key is to tap into some kind of relevancy to your customers.

It can be done. Cat food, for example, is far from a high-ticket item. It may be hard to imagine cat food purchasers registering with an online affinity group. Yet Purina has a wonderful and very popular affinity Web site for cat lovers, filled with cat care tips, vets who offer advice online, and so on. Purina's genius lay in recognizing that cat lovers share certain values with one another. (That is why strangers who find themselves holding their cats together in the waiting room at the vet's office will talk with one another right away—they have something important in common.) This commonality gave Purina the opportunity to use the Internet to create a link to their best customers, making the Web site into a source of data about the number of cats in a household, purchase patterns, cats' eating habits, and so on.

If you sell a low-cost and commodity-like product or service—bread, for example-you'll want to do some research to figure out how you can become more relevant to your customers—that is, how you can tap into their values. If Kraft can do it and Purina can do it, so can you. Then use what you learn to build a frequent-customer program based on those shared values.

THE FIVE QUINTILES

Once you've gathered your customer data and ranked your customers from those who generate the greatest sales volume down to those who generate the least, divide them into five equal groups—quintiles. Each quintile, by definition, contains an equal number of customers, so, for example, if your entire database consists of 160,000 customers, each quintile will contain $160,000 \div 5 = 32,000$ customers, or 20 percent of your customer count.

The top quintile—which I refer to as quintile 1, or simply Q_1—contains your highest-volume customers. Obviously, this is your most important group of customers. The next-highest group, Q_2, consists of your second-highest-volume customers, and so on down to Q_5, customers who buy the least from you.

There's generally a very strong, almost linear relationship between quintiles and sales contribution. This is probably not surprising—as I have noted, it's a variation on the traditional 80/20 rule. In practice, I've found that the Q_1 customers usually account for somewhere between 50 and 80 percent of a company's sales, with the average figure somewhere around 60 percent. This means that each of your Q_1 customers is worth about three times as much as the average customer.

Does the same pattern hold in e-commerce? Data are scanty, but existing evidence suggests that, if anything, the pattern may be even stronger than in traditional retail. According to a September 2000 InterActive Consumers Study from Cyber Dialogue, the top 20 percent of online shoppers are responsible for *nearly 90 percent* of total sales.

My quintile management studies also have revealed that most companies make virtually all their profits from sales to their Q_1 and Q_2

customers. They generally break even on sales to Q_3 customers and actually lose money when selling to Q_4 and Q_5 customers (when full market costs are charged). Do you find this startling? Most business-people do.

Of course, this kind of analysis is also much more work than simply lumping all your customers together. However, what it suggests is so important that it's worth the time, effort, and expense involved.

The five simple charts labeled Figure 7-1 through Figure 7-5 show vividly how the quintiles should—and should not—be related to your marketing expenditures.

Figure 7-1 shows the typical pattern of sales contribution by quintile—with much greater sales volume being generated by Q_1 than by the other four quintiles. In Figure 7-2, I have inserted a trend line that emphasizes the relationship between quintiles and sales.

Actually, the problem is more serious than this. In Figure 7-3, the dotted line represents contribution to profit by quintile. Q_1 makes an even greater contribution to your bottom line than its sales percentage would suggest, whereas Q_5 actually *costs* you money.

Figure 7-4 illustrates some of the consequences of the way most companies currently do business. The solid line that stretches horizontally across the graph represents typical marketing expenditures per quintile. Yes, they are flat—since most companies today don't segment their customers by quintile and therefore are spending marketing money equally across the entire range. Note the large shaded area at the

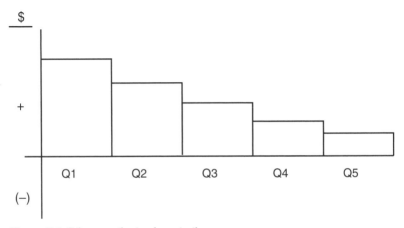

Figure 7-1 Sales contribution by quintile.

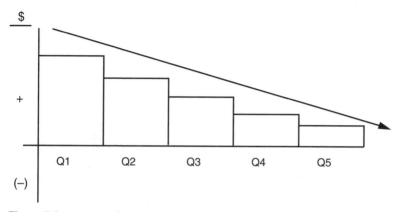

Figure 7-2 Average sales contribution by quintile.

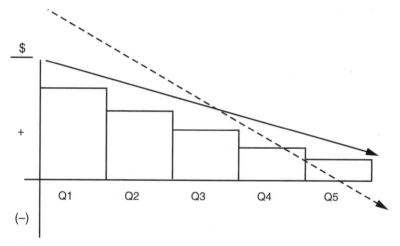

Figure 7-3 Contribution to profit by quintile.

lower right-hand side of the graph. It represents the gap between dollars spent marketing to the lower quintiles and the low or negative profit earned from those groups. *These are wasted expenditures— marketing costs that yield no profit and are a pure loss to your business.*

Figure 7-5 shows what you need to do differently. Here, the wasted marketing dollars have been shifted (as represented by the shaded area at upper left) to where they will do the most good—to Q_1 and Q_2. Now the marketing money will serve to attract, retain, and maximize sales from your best customers rather than being thrown away on your worst. And notice that the size of the shaded area in this chart is about the same as

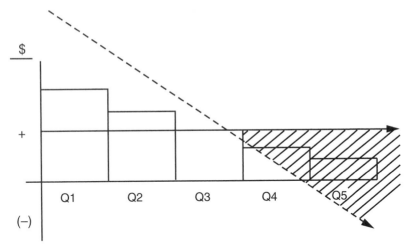

Figure 7-4 Typical marketing expenditures by quintile.

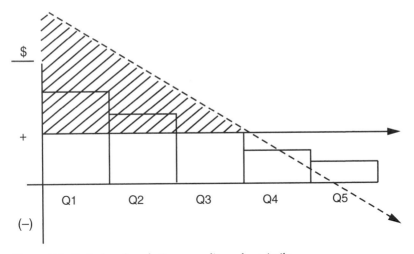

Figure 7-5 Redeployed marketing expenditures by quintile.

the shaded area in Figure 7-4. Quintile marketing doesn't (necessarily) involve increasing your marketing budget—it involves redistributing the same money so as to give you the "best bang for your buck."

Okay, then. Suppose you've got your quintiles defined and you have a way to communicate with them. Now what? Well, so far, what you have is a behavioral relationship. You know *what* they're doing, but that's Old and New Economy data. In the Next Economy, you need to know *why*. So let's ask them.

The wonderful thing about Q_1 and Q_2 customers is that they already have an important relationship with your brand. What you want to know is what the relationship is and how to expand it. Because you are already perceived to be one of their favorites, they are more responsive to research. Ask for more information about what's important to them so that you can qualify them into want segments and understand which other brands are important in their life. These answers will go a long way toward building relevancy into your business strategy.

I started this chapter with a generalized description of your company's best and worst customers. As you can now see, these are really descriptions of your Q_1 and Q_5 customers. Let's take a closer look at how customers in each of the quintiles tend to behave and how you need to respond to them as the custodian of your brand's value. I have found that every quintile has a holistic relationship with a given brand, meaning that there's a natural and effective way to work with each one.

Let's start at the bottom of the customer pile. Customers in Q_5 are price-driven. They are cherry pickers, buying only very selectively and usually at discount prices, and they generally belong to a smaller household—therefore, they tend to make smaller purchases. They have a minimal relationship with your brand and are need-based rather than want-based buyers in their purchasing decisions. As a result, profit margins on sales to Q_5 are really small, often nonexistent. These customers are usually driven into stores and onto Web sites by Old Economy mass-marketing tools, such as run-of-press newspaper and magazine ads or commercials on network radio or TV.

Ironically, because of the way they purchase, we often subsidize their patronage, using margin dollars from the Q_1, Q_2, and Q_3 customers, when common sense would dictate that it should be the other way around!

Often these Q_5 relationships are maintained for other reasons. You recall our conversation on oligopoly breakeven points, where volume is critical to overhead absorption. A common response from the financial group is that without these people, the cost of the company will be borne by the remaining four segments, thereby placing their profitability in jeopardy. This has not been my experience.

Trading in Q_5 for Q_3 or Q_4 customers will redistribute your quintiles and move the profitability of the business forward—big time. The very nature of the quintiles will change and although the relative contribution of Q_5 customers to your business will still place them as Q_5 customers, and by definition not supported, the absolute value of the Q_5 contribution can be managed upward as a by-product of focusing on the top-producing customers. As I've said, some customers you don't want. However, if you have to have them, at least make them pay their own way.

As you modify the quintile programs each year, the customer mix will change. There will always be a fifth quintile, and although their value to the company can be enhanced, it's just not worth the effort to do so directly.

Perhaps you're wondering whether Q_5 consumers tend to be drawn from the ranks of the less affluent. Actually, income has little to do directly with quintiles. The same customer will fall into a different quintile for different products because the same category that represents a want for me may represent a need for you. For example, for some people, a car is a need; all they are interested in is a stripped-down, economical, plain-Jane car that will get them where they're going for minimal cost. For others, it's a want: They window-shop for cars, daydream about their favorite models, and look forward to the time when they can afford the sports car of their fantasies.

This is one of the reasons demographics doesn't work as a practical marketing tool. The person who spends every penny of disposable money on his or her car may be a Q_1 customer for cars, even though his or her income may be relatively low. *Demographics can't tell you this—only psychographics and quintile management can.*

Thus some people who fall into Q_5 for some categories of products and services may have high incomes and high levels of education. Paper goods, for example, may be bought on a commodity basis by affluent people. Sometimes the same person who will spend $25,000 on an antique vase won't spent 25 cents more for a roll of toilet paper—and she prides herself on both choices.

So quintiles don't work across categories. The identity of the customers in your five quintiles depends on the relationships you have and want to have with customers and what they want from both your category and your brand. These factors will be very different from one category to another.

The customer in Q_4 is similar to the customer in Q_5 but has a larger economic base for your product. (Remember that quintiles are based on the volume of their purchases from you.) This customer, like the Q_5

customer, is a cherry picker, price-oriented, and mass-oriented, but she is buying for a large household or in large quantities. This tends to make her especially price-oriented and comparison-oriented.

Because of the volume, she can be an important part of your overhead absorption, so I counsel my clients to leave the Q_4 customer alone. I don't mind trading off a Q_5 individual, but a volume user who has no desire for a relationship is still a volume user.

What stops her from moving up to Q_3 could be any number of things. Sometimes it's simply the household budget. Sometimes the category has no relevance to her. Sometimes the geography gets in the way of the frequency of purchase. It doesn't really matter because Q_4 customers are exposed to those mass elements of the marketing strategy we still use in the Next Economy when our big price events are on. In fact, we only use mass programs to include her in the reach so that we can make the sales numbers that in turn absorb the overhead.

The Q_3 customer is a short-list customer. In her life, there are two or three brands that she is willing to buy in a given category, and she will buy whatever happens to be available or attractively priced from this short list. If you want to reach more Q_3 customers, your objective is to be on their short list. Incentive programs work well with Q_3 customers—programs such as a double-point program or a gift-with-purchase program. Sometimes offering a Q_3 customer a guest benefits program—for example, a free temporary pass into a airline's private lounge—can inspire her to upgrade into a Q_1 or Q_2 buyer. Another example might be a special pass to the "private" parts of your Web site for a limited period of time. Never give her for free what she ought to earn (through higher-volume purchases)—just let her taste it.

Your ultimate objective is to become the leading brand for this person not by continually subsidizing her purchases through special deals and discounts but by delighting her through unique and valuable offerings. Such incentives can help her graduate to Q_1 or Q_2 by eliminating other brands from her short list, thereby bumping up her sales level and importance to you.

Your relationship with the Q_2 customer is one of preference. She may still be short-list shopping, but you are her preferred brand. Therefore, you won't get *all* of her business; occasionally a competitor will incent her enough to get her to try its brand. If you're smart, however, your Q_2 marketing strategies are retention-oriented. They might include such programs as customized catalogs, private-shopper programs, special lounge access, unique intranets that can be reached from your Internet site with private passwords, valuable benefits earned through high-purchase volume, and personalized, one-to-one messages—for example, a letter from the company president thanking the customer for her patronage and giving her some kind of special gift.

Q_2 customers are more important to business in the Next Economy because fewer customers will be shopping for fewer products and services. A Q_2 loss is a serious problem, yet we often focus on retaining Q_1 and providing incentives to Q_3 customers. Our recommendation is not to differentiate significantly between Q_1 and Q_2 programs but certainly leave a few on the table that make her ascension to Q_1 worthwhile.

The customer in Q_1 is brand-loyal. There's no more short-list shopping for the Q_1 customer. She'll shop elsewhere only when she can't buy from you for some reason beyond her control. The strategy for managing your Q_1 customers is rewards. Offer surprise benefits on top of earned benefits—congratulate and thank your Q_1 customer as often as possible. Pamper her with preferred shopper programs and give her free product or service upgrades without being asked. Assign her a private and uniquely identifying code number to speed up her shopping—using the code number, you know where to ship her purchases and how she likes them delivered and charged without your asking. Perhaps you'll want to offer her subsidized patronage, in which you pay for shipping, gift wrap, and send anything anywhere. Make this a personal experience. And let her buy from a "private cache"—no standing in line.

Food store operators take heed of this last point. Why install a "ten items or less" express line in your store, thereby rewarding your Q_5 customers? Instead, try a "one hundred items or more" line staffed with twice the personnel to speed and enhance service for your best customers.

And make sure that at every point of contact with the Q_1 customer, everyone in your company knows that this is a loyal customer. Provide her with a different color credit card, and code her shipping labels so that everyone who handles the package knows they're dealing with a best customer. Invest in caller ID that tells the customer-care specialists who's on the line automatically. Calls from a Q_1 customer go automatically to a special group of "personal care" reps.

The key is to delight your Q_1 customers—to focus constantly on what you can do for them, never vice versa. Hertz Gold Club is a great example of how this can work. Club members have only to show a valid driver's license to pick up their car. No counter service is required. Your name often appears on a marquee, your spot number is indicated, the trunk is open, and you're out of there.

Bloomingdale's Preferred Customer Program is another example. Customers who have spent considerable dollars with Bloomies get called by the store when new products in their favorite brands arrive. Using outbound telemarketing, I'm guessing that the company's conversion rate with Q_1 and Q_2 customers must be in the 40 to 50 percent range.

The airlines' frequent flyer programs have long segregated their best customers and treated them quite differently—all in the open. When I hear from a client that there is a resistance to implement a quintile strategy for fear of alienating their other customers, I always point to the airlines. While not known for their service, the airlines have figured out how to overtly pamper their best customers right under the noses of their worst customers. In so doing, they are educating us all on how much chutzpah customers can tolerate. I know of no one who has switched airlines because they couldn't get on with the Platinum folks. Thus we've learned that as customers, there will be differences in treatment and that, overall, business and their customers have a reciprocal contract with each other that carries with it differing expectations.

Naturally, in every business category, everybody wants to capture the Q_1 and Q_2 customers. The intensity of the battle at this end of the spectrum is huge because the customers are so valuable; in fact, every customer in Q_1 has a profit value equivalent to 30 to 50 Q_5 customers. Therefore, shifting a Q_1 customer from one brand to another is a huge victory. Some smart companies are already tailoring acquisition strategies to get Q_1 customers to change brands. They are offering, for example, to honor all the benefits customers have earned from other brands. And they are offering VIP credits, saying, in effect, "Sign up to change brands, and we'll instantly give you special-privileges experiences that others have to wait for and earn." It's like the signing bonuses paid to sports stars.

By the same token, there are customers one doesn't want—particularly Q_5 people. Now I'm not suggesting discriminating against these folks. Simply ignoring them will work most effectively. Inevitably they will either continue to plod along as occasional players or move to a competitive offering that discounts more heavily. This is just another reason to use price discounting more judiciously. As we saw earlier, it rarely sustains customers. Now you know why.

Therefore, a competitive acquisition program focused on potential Q_1 and Q_2 customers is one of the most important weapons you'll need to win in the Next Economy. In a nutshell, the strategy is:

- Discourage Q_5 customers.
- Ignore Q_4 customers.
- Do battle for Q_3 customers.
- Wage all-out war to capture and retain Q_1 and Q_2 customers.

THE PERSISTENCE OF MASS MARKETING

Once you get used to thinking about your customer base in quintile terms, it seems obvious that marketing and advertising *must* be driven by a focus on the Q_1 and Q_2 customers. Yet most companies fail completely to practice this. Most marketing expenditures remain perversely level across all quintiles largely because our marketing and advertising programs continue to be mass-driven. We reward advertising agencies and media companies that deliver "eyeballs" at the lowest cost per thousand (CPM), which immediately pushes us toward the lower quintiles rather than the higher ones. And we create marketing programs that are designed to appeal to middle-of-the-road customers—which, by definition, are Q_3 customers.

As a result, most of our marketing efforts have no special relevance to our most important customers. Thus we are treating our worst customers the same as our best customers and doing little or nothing to reward our best customers for their patronage and loyalty.

In the Next Economy, these issues will be intensified. In most businesses, fewer marketing dollars will be available in the Next Economy than in the past. Why? Remember that most marketing budgets are set as a percentage of sales. This means that in the softening environment of the naughts, marketing budgets also will be softening. Thus the question of how to target those marketing dollars most effectively will be more important than ever.

There's not enough audience discrimination in the mass media to effectively isolate your Q_1 and Q_2 customers. When you buy space or time in newspapers or on broadcast TV, you're buying a fairly broad (i.e., mass-market) audience reach. And as we've seen, the commonly used measures of advertising efficiency tend to force us into a lowest-cost mode. Cable is somewhat better in its focus, and for some product categories, narrowcasting cable can work.

In the Next Economy, the whole concept of mass targeting makes little sense. It's a lowest-common-denominator concept that does nothing to identify and focus on our best customers, instead wasting resources on millions of people who will never repay the investment.

I don't mean to say that network TV advertising and other forms of mass communication are completely without value. There are some Old Economy companies that have built success on such a huge scale that they need mass communication just to keep their vast markets churning.

Coca-Cola, for example, is a successful brand built on an Old Economy model. Such a business can't really be run on a Next Economy basis in its existing form. However, who will be brave enough to take the chance on redefining the Coke strategy for the Next Economy?

By contrast, a brand such as Gatorade can be specifically formulated for particular needs and therefore can be marketed in a highly targeted way toward Q_1 and Q_2 customers. The same could be said of, for example, a special variety of orange juice that is fortified with calcium or iron. Coke, by definition, can't be marketed this way. The Coca-Cola Company can and does create new brands with Next Economy qualities. However, the original Coke brand can only get bigger by selling more in countries that are a generation behind North America in terms of consumption.

But don't worry—Coke won't be going out of business any time soon. It is a great brand and a great company. The same is true of some other mass-market products. Take the big beer brands, for example. They've all been going after the same vast audience using mass advertising in media that beer drinkers favor—televised sports in particular. Only one or two market giants (Anheuser-Busch, Miller) are likely to win a battle like that. They have the most to spend, and a mass communication war always comes down to sheer firepower. Nonetheless, the Q_1 customer for beer can be narrowly defined. That's why local breweries and specialty brands are exploding in sales. Thus the "little guy" is not necessarily a loser, if he focuses effectively on the right quintile.

There are also specific times when mass communication tools make sense even for a brand that is moving toward a Next Economy model.

You might still need to reach a large swatch of Q_4 and Q_5 customers when it's necessary to artificially stimulate sales and build temporary consumption. For example, if you misjudge demand for a particular product and overpurchase, it may be necessary to reach out to the Q_4 and Q_5 customer in order to clear out inventory. Sometimes, you just can't make your sales budget for the quarter and need a temporary sales fix. Here, too, mass marketing may be in order.

The point is that for most companies, mass marketing will be done on a tactical basis, not as a regular strategy. Remember: Such tactics may build temporary consumption, but they do nothing to build your brand equity.

NIBBLED TO DEATH

The Old Economy isn't vanishing altogether. Neither is the New Economy. However, the Next Economy is becoming more and more dominant, and it will determine the next big winners on the business battlefield. Next Economy companies gradually will siphon off market share from the big Old Economy winners, slowly undermining the power and dominance of the old oligopolies. Specialty drinks gradually will erode the dominance of Coke and Pepsi; microbrews, imported beers, and other unique beverages gradually will steal share from Budweiser and Miller.

Brands that succeeded in the Old Economy by virtue of their economies of scale and efficiency of buying are all vulnerable to the Next Economy strategy of personalization. Since most consumer and B2B brands dominate their respective markets in this manner, they are the most vulnerable to the change in market dynamics that is around the corner.

By 2010, it will be very clear that the folks who have focused on their best customers through quintile marketing will be pulling ahead in terms of profits, having built stronger and deeper relationships between customers and their brands. And those who continue to rely on mass marketing and mass communication will find themselves being nibbled to death by ducks.

8

The Four R's

Let's review what we've learned so far. Businesses that depend on traditional marketing, as we've seen, are in trouble—big trouble. The difficulties your business has probably been experiencing—marginal sales growth, declining customer loyalty, and weakening profit margins—aren't due to mistakes you've made (although, like most businesses, you've probably made your share). They are symptoms of a deeper problem, precursors of a major business upheaval that's just around the corner. It is the inevitable result of converging social, demographic, and economic trends that will bring us, within the next few years, into an intense period of negative growth and deflation that I call the Next Economy.

Few business are prepared to cope with this impending upheaval. Many are still attempting to market their goods and services using to the old formula of the Four P's, an increasingly outdated and ineffective set of marketing tools. Some are mired in the structural problems inherent in the traditional, pyramid-like system of brand management, which places a premium on the short-term sales fix rather than on the building of long-term brand equity. Most have yet to learn how to focus on their best and most profitable customers, and others are still trying to use traditional demographic measurements to understand consumers. Each of these, as we've seen, is a mistake that will fail to help prepare your business for the Next Economy.

We have also seen that the legacy of the New Economy is that businesses built exclusively on speed or information are not economically sustainable because their business models do not provide enough of a benefit to a wide enough group of people to sustain the costs of operations. Their reliance on equity financing, scalability, and low prices is based on the false presumption that people wanted more speed and information and that this want could sustain a premium. Wrong on both counts. Speed and information are needs, not wants. Both are necessities of the New Economy. But as we've seen, there's no margin in needs.

However, there are new directions—new ways of thinking—that hold out hope for marketers entering this challenging new environment. One key is to begin defining customers not by demographics—the traditional aspects of age, income, and education that marketers have long been trained to examine—but rather by psychographics—the values, concerns, and wishes that define what customers *want* rather than what they *need*. Another is to abandon the common assumption that "all customers are created equal." Instead, I have urged you to explore the power of quintile management. This approach to marketing divides the customers of any business into five segments, defined by their varying degrees of loyalty to your brand or banner and by their varying profitability for your business. As we saw, your most loyal, affluent, and brand-aware customers make up quintiles 1 and 2—the top 40 percent of your customer base—and they constitute your most important and profitable market. If you understand what makes them buy and focus your marketing on them, your business will have a chance to grow. Otherwise, you'll probably flounder, selling on a catch-as-catch-can basis with little assurance that today's customers will still be around tomorrow.

So far, so good. However, assuming that you know your target market—the quintile 1 and 2 customers you most want to reach—how do you create a marketing strategy that is meaningful to them? Since the traditional Four P's—Price, Product, Place, and Promotion—no longer work, a new marketing toolbox is necessary, one that recognizes and responds to the realities of the new marketplace. I call it the Four R's.

The Four P's of the Old Economy were concerned with managing the flow of goods and services from the manufacturer to the consumer. The New Economy was concerned with managing technology and speed. The Next Economy will be concerned with managing every point of customer contact in a consistent and reinforcing manner that is capable of building profitable relationships between brands and their best customers. The Four R's are therefore a critical third part of my brand-building prescription for the Next Economy.

THE NEW MARKETING EQUATION

Let's start by recalling the marketing equation:

$$\text{Brand value} = \frac{\text{equity}}{\text{price}}$$

As I explained earlier, *brand value* is what your product or service is worth. *Price* is, simply, what it costs. The difference between the two is *equity*. And the real purpose of marketing is to *build equity*—to leave the brand with a more powerful franchise and a stronger customer relationship than when you inherited or created it.

The greater the perceived equity in a product or service, the greater is the brand value—and the higher the Price can safely go. Today, in most industries, equity is no longer carrying its weight—in fact, it is constantly being eroded. We've seen the reasons why. The death of the Four P's is at the heart of the problem. When it's virtually impossible to differentiate your brand on the basis of Product, Place, or Promotion— as is true today—there's no foundation in the Four P's for building Brand Equity. This means that, from the old formula, only Price remains. And any business whose marketing strategy is built around ever-decreasing prices is a dying business.

A new version of the marketing equation is needed, one that reflects the marketing realities of today and tomorrow: the need for businesses to rely on *fewer* but *better* customers, the fact that people today buy products and services not because they *need* them but because they *want* them, and the necessary future management structure of marketing, which must move from a pyramidal model to a collaborative one.

Here's the new equation:

$$\text{Brand value} = \frac{\text{Relationships, Retrenchment, Relevancy, Rewards}}{\text{Price}}$$

As you can see, the simple term *equity* from the old Marketing Equation has been (figuratively) exploded into a four-part expression—

Relationships, Retrenchment, Relevancy, Rewards. These are the Four R's—today's four basic building blocks for constructing a meaningful strategy that profitably builds brand equity. I place these Four R's *over* Price in the equation to show clearly the relationship among them: As your strategic use of the Four R's increases, so does your brand value relative to price. The greater your brand equity, the greater the value of your brand in the eyes of customers, and the higher the price your product or service can bear—and the better your business's profit margins.

Each of the Four R's, in turn, is associated with two *Core Competencies*—fundamental skills around which successful approaches for differentiating your business can be developed. The Four R's and the Eight Core Competencies associated with them encapsulate the eight ways that marketing can build brand value in the Next Economy.

Now let's take a closer look at each of the Four R's and the Core Competencies associated with them.

THE FIRST R: RELATIONSHIPS

The Four P's of the old marketing toolbox placed the individual transaction at the heart of marketing. In its day, this wasn't a bad approach. In the need-based world of the 1950s, the main challenge for marketers was to let consumers know about the availability of their products. Once that happened, the powerful force of consumer demand driven by the baby boomers could take over, and when one sale was finished, there was always another customer waiting in line.

Today's marketing must be focused not on individual transactions but on building strong, growing connections between our businesses and our best customers. The most meaningful measurement is *share of customer spending* (SOCS). Whatever you sell—clothing, computers, CDs, food, or financial services—your goal should be to become your customers' supplier of choice for those products or services. It's a matter of focusing on the target customers rather than on one sale at a time.

In the Old and New Economies, the sale was the end of the relationship, the culmination of the huge marketing investment that preceded its occurrence. In the Next Economy, the sale is the beginning of the relationship. In an era of fewer customers, the best will be celebrated as often as possible.

Thus a crucial strategy for building brand value in the Next Economy is to forge a unique *Relationship* with the members of your target market. I have found that there are two Core Competencies that can be effectively employed in doing this: *Service* and *Experience*. I will explain both.

Service

The quality of service, of course, is a long-standing concern of almost every business. There are dozens of books that purport to explain the secrets of "knock-your-socks-off service," and there are hundreds of consultants and trainers who promise to instill good service practices into your organization.

As consumers, we all have our favorite stories of great service, like the legendary—probably apocryphal—manager at Nordstrom's who cheerfully accepted the return of a set of tires for a full refund—even though Nordstrom's doesn't sell tires. On the other side, we all have stories of the times we've been victimized by horrible service. (Sadly, these kinds of stories seem to be far more numerous today.)

However, although service is much talked about, many in business don't understand what it really means. Traditionally, service refers to shopping assistance. In a retail store, it means providing a competent, knowledgeable salesclerk who understands the merchandise available, can locate it for the customer, and can ring up the sale accurately and quickly. Online, it means having a Web site that leads the customer easily and accurately through the steps needed to load up his or her shopping cart and make the transaction using a credit card or other secure means of payment, with no unpleasant surprises and access to live help as needed.

All this is necessary and important, of course—and often lacking. But there's much more to service as a marketing strategy. The fact is that service is the single biggest challenge facing North American business. Customers generally are disappointed with the level of service they now receive, whether offline or online. And when they complain about service, they aren't necessarily referring to the quality of the sales help in a retail environment. Instead, they are referring to *the entire encounter with your company and your brand*, from the moment they first consider making a purchase right through the experience of using the product or service. If service is to become an effective marketing tool for your company, you'll need to examine, rethink, and redesign every step in this process. *Every customer contact point is a serviceable opportunity—a medium for delighting her.*

Of course, improving the quality of the selling process may be an important part of the solution. Retailers desperately need to hire and develop people who know not only what you have to sell but also how to use and combine your offerings to meet the customer's wants—both the overt ones that drive the customer into your store in the first place and the more subtle, hidden ones that she may not even fully realize herself. And e-tailers need to create Web sites that encourage customers to explore related categories or products and services as well as appropriate ways to upgrade their purchases with accessories or add-ons. The business-to-business (B2B) segment has understood this for years.

Thus great service means not only being courteous and efficient in answering customer questions and closing the sale, but also being proactive about discovering and fulfilling the customers' wants. The sales dialogue must include not only the classic, magic words "Please" and "Thank you" but also lines like these:

"If you want the best beaches in February, you should consider Mexico as well as Florida. We have three favorite resorts that set aside premium rooms for our clients at special prices—let me show you some pictures."

"If your company plans to do a lot of graphic work with these new computers, you should really consider larger monitors. Here's a new line of affordable, large-screen monitors we've just started carrying—they got a great review in the top computer magazine last month."

"We're getting some handsome brass lamps in next week that will really work with those end tables—may I call you when they arrive?"

For retailers, service means training your associates to understand how to quickly qualify a particular customer and how to use this to guide the associate's interaction with the customer. You can't offer state-of-the-art service unless you know both the inventory and the customer's wants. There's no reason not to know the former. The latter requires experience and empathy, and it can be learned. To make this kind of proactive service possible, more knowledgeable, professional, better-trained salespeople are needed. (And yes, you'll probably need to pay them more than you're paying now. They'll be worth every penny and then some.)

Salespeople should function as *sales consultants*. It's not just a semantic difference. The traditional sales associate works for you; the sales consultant is working for the customer. As customers notice and enjoy the difference, the truly professional sales consultant becomes, in and of herself, an important reason why customers will come back repeatedly to your brand or banner.

Beyond upgrading your sales staff, however, there are dozens of other ways your business can make buying from you more enjoyable and delightful for your customers (and for you, more profitable). To decide which ones are right for you, spend time experiencing your business the way your customers experience it, and let your ideas for change be driven by their wants—especially the wants of your customers in quintiles 1 and 2.

Nordstrom's great reputation is well deserved; it does in-store service phenomenally well. In a different way, so do some of the warehouse stores, such as Home Depot, which provides customers with huge shopping carts, freedom to roam aisles loaded with every conceivable home improvement product, and unobtrusive but knowledgeable salespeople who are ready to help answer questions, look for merchandise, or solve problems.

By contrast, the big-box home electronics stores *should* be great at service; their product mix lends itself to all kinds of proactive customer-service opportunities. Imagine if the salesperson at your local electronics store took a few minutes to ask about your favorite kinds of music and the size and furnishings of your family room—and helped you customize your choice of stereo speakers accordingly. You'd probably become a customer for life.

Unfortunately, none of the large electronics chains (to my knowledge) have mastered this art. However, it's what keeps the small chain store, such as New York's J&R Music World) and the single-store retailer alive. Consider, for example, the family-owned Fortunoff retail chain. This business is so wedded to service and expertise that it refuses to build any store located further than a few hours' drive from the family homes in New York. If the company's managers can't provide hands-on supervision and leadership, they don't want to be involved.

Computer retailing, like electronics retailing, is an area where service has not been used sufficiently as a strategy. This is a major reason why consumers in these areas have turned more and more to direct manufacturers on the Web to get electronics products from knowledgeable people who both build and sell them. Historically, computer retailers have acted merely as intermediaries rather than adding value through service. Had they invested in service, computer sales could be driving retailing today, at a profit. Instead, they're having the opposite effect, often at a loss.

By contrast, Dell and Gateway have pioneered the art of excellent customer service online. Their process lets the customer design his or her own personal computer, first selecting from a handful of standard desktop or laptop models and then choosing components that closely match his or her personal needs, from a particular size and type of monitor to specific choices of memory size, software packages, and so on. At every stage in the buying process, it's easy to click on a help button and get easy-to-understand, plain-English explanations for technical terms as well as shopping advice. And when the process of configuring the computer is completed, Dell will manufacture the machine to the customer's specifications and ship it to his or her door, usually within a few days. You can do it all just as easily by phone.

Of course, Amazon is becoming as well known for its online service as Nordstrom is for its retail service. Once you've shopped Amazon's Web site, you get a personal greeting. Place an order, and you get a thank-you confirmation by e-mail. When the product is shipped, you're notified. You get follow-up e-mails with suggested purchases on the same or similar topics. And it's all seamless and unobtrusive. It works because it's not just information but knowledge-based service that adds value to your relationship with the Amazon brand.

For packaged-goods companies and other businesses that deal with consumers indirectly, the service competency is even more critical. Such businesses have no direct influence on the quality of the service received by the customer during the transaction. To compensate for this, they need to establish a strong service capability *during consumption.*

Today, technology can be a crucial ally. The Web and 800-number telephone services provide excellent vehicles for enhancing and building your reputation for service. For those who need it, outside help is also available. Call centers are popping up all over the place as manufacturers come to realize the important role of after-sales service in the business-to-customer (B2C) space. Once again, this is something B2B marketers have understood for years.

As I mentioned earlier, most people have a favorite service story. Here's one I like. A friend—call him Mark—received an attractive sterling silver ball point pen manufactured by Parker as a gift and used it with pleasure for years. One day, he dropped it on a hard floor and found, to his chagrin, that a plastic piece inside the pen had broken, preventing the point-retractor mechanism from working smoothly.

An associate on the other end of Parker's 800 line offered to send a special mailing tube for Mark to use to return the pen for repair. He did, expecting a small charge for the service. Instead, he received back the pen in a week's time with a little note saying that there would be no charge for the repair. And in addition to the repair, he found that the decorative grooves in the pen's silver housing had been thoroughly cleaned and a new ink cartridge had been provided.

In literal terms, Mark had never been a Parker customer—his pen had been a gift, not a purchase. But ever since experiencing that small sample of the company's service, he has told that story over and over—and recommended Parker pens to everyone he knows.

Although service traditionally has been defined as occurring before or during the transaction, increasingly service occurs *after* the transaction. A lasting customer relationship doesn't end when the sale is completed—that's when it starts. This is why after-sales service is crucially important. It can take many forms:

- Prompt, expert, and courteous delivery and setup of the product in the home by delivery people who are knowledgeable enough to answer basic questions about the product.
- A phone call to the customer from a sales associate 1 week after delivery.
- Technical support, provided weeks or months after the purchase, by professionals who are smart, fast, and polite.

- Knowledgeable, courteous, prompt, and generous handling of repairs, replacements, and upgrades, whether covered by warranty or not.
- Newsletters and Web sites that keep customers abreast of new developments that might affect them, such as new ways to consume the product or use the service.

Chances are good that your business is providing these on a haphazard basis—if at all. This is not good enough any longer.

The Internet can be a powerful tool for improved follow-up service. One recent Dell customer (I'll call him Tim) had a small but tricky problem with his new laptop. It took three phone calls for Tim to resolve the problem with the help of a Dell technician. But Tim was impressed by the speed and efficiency of the process. Each time he called Dell, he was connected with the service department within 5 minutes. And each service rep had instant access to notes from Dell's previous conversations with Tim, so there was no need to review what had already been tried. Rather than having to lug his computer to a repair shop or crate it for a 2-week stay at a service center, Tim got it fixed online quickly and at no cost to him.

Thus, in the new marketing environment, the definition of service is changing. Service now includes not only the buying experience but also the consumption experience.

Consequently, where the Four P's were concerned only with the transaction ("How do we make the sale?"), the Four R's go beyond the transaction ("How do we make a Q_1 customer for life?"). As long as the customer is using your product or service—a week, a month, a year after the purchase—he or she is still involved in a relationship with your brand, which can be source of delight or irritation to him or her. Don't blow the game in the fourth quarter by ignoring the customer as soon as her check clears. It's a marriage, not a one-night stand.

This is particularly important for packaged goods manufacturers. Too many have abandoned their customer service responsibilities, abdicating them to retailers. And as their marketing investments have followed this change in priorities, fewer dollars are available to spend on consumers. What has been spent is generally irrelevant to future purchase decisions and therefore fails to build the brand. Marketing moneys invested in 800 numbers, online expertise, and other forms of postpurchase service are true builders of brand equity and pay huge dividends for years to come. And yes, they can be funded from mass advertising budgets.

Experience

The second Core Competency within the Relationship strategy is *Experience*. Companies that build their business around this competency strive to make the experience of transacting and using the product or service absolutely unique, delightful, and rewarding.

Of course, like Service, this isn't a new concept—just a new perspective. Like all of the Core Competencies, they can be seen at work in great businesses throughout history. In tomorrow's marketing environment, however, they take on a new importance.

Let's begin with retail. People have always loved unique shopping experiences. At its best, shopping has always been a social, sensual, and aesthetic experience as well as an economic one. In the Middle Ages, merchants and customers traveled hundreds of miles to savor the sights, smells, sounds, and textures of the great trade fairs in Bologna and Frankfurt; in the cities of the Renaissance, wonderful shopping streets and bazaars were established where everyone from nobles to peasants could bargain for the clothes, foodstuffs, crafts, and artworks flowing into Europe from Asia, Africa, and the New World, and to this day, the names of great retail streets, from Fifth Avenue to Rodeo Drive, evoke an atmosphere of excitement, surprise, and glamour that appeals to everyone. Great business minds have always understood, at least intuitively, the importance of both the psychology and the physiology of buying.

Today, retailers must relearn the art of delighting the customer by providing a unique, memorable, and enjoyable buying experience. The theater of the store is an important contact point to manage, and it can build strong loyalty and clear differentiation with customers who find most products duplicated in most competing stores. Experience is not a merchant's issue. This will be covered shortly under Merchandising. Nor is experience Service. It is the sensory reaction to the act of shopping or consuming.

Retail experience need not be exotic or luxurious to register with customers. In its own way, the low-technology club store with its warehouse look and oversized shopping carts is a differentiating experience millions of people enjoy. As is the lowly flea market, where browsing for gems amid junk and haggling over nickels is all part of the fun. Delighting the customer may begin with the simplest of amenities: a free cup of fresh coffee; a comfortable, well-located sitting area for a tired spouse; a library-style table at which bookstore browsers can stretch out with the first chapter of a new novel; an outlet for fast food conveniently located inside a big-box store.

There's no single formula for a great buying Experience. (If there were, it would become routine—the opposite of exciting and compelling.) Your challenge is to find ways to delight the customer that make the Experience of buying from you different from that of buying from your competitors. After all, in today's business environment, everyone can offer the same merchandise—and probably does. Therefore, making the buying experience unique is a powerful tool that gives the customer a reason to think first of your brand or banner.

There are a number of retailers that, with much fanfare, have made the Experience central to their marketing strategy. The Disney and Warner Brothers studio stores, Nike's sports-themed Niketown, and the enormous Tourneau Corner emporium for watches, clocks, and jewelry are all examples. So is Sephora, the successful French cosmetics chain, famous for its huge, flatteringly lit stores with dozens of brands of makeup and fragrance, most available on open shelves for customers to see, handle, and test.

Another example is Bass Pro Shops, one of the fastest-growing suppliers of outdoor gear in the world. Fishing and hunting are big business. Over 35 million Americans participate each year, spending nearly $60 billion on travel, clothes, equipment, and related expenses. And when they're not thigh deep in an icy stream or camping in a remote pine forest, American anglers and hunters spend their free time thinking about their hobby—planning their next trip, bragging about the last one, and especially shopping for the latest and best equipment.

Several successful businesses have been built around the retail fishing and hunting markets, including Cabela's (mainly in the midwest), Orvis (in Vermont), and Maine's L.L. Bean. Most sell their products both by catalog and in retail outlets. Bass Pro Shops, based in Springfield, Missouri, is perhaps the most innovative of them all. Their not-so-secret weapon? Creation of a special buying experience that captures the magic of the outdoors both for avid sportsmen and sportswomen and for novices ready to be hooked. The flagship Bass store in Springfield covers 300,000 square feet. Naturally, it carries virtually every imaginable type of fishing and hunting equipment, from boats and motor homes to tents, camping gear, clothes, guns, rods, reels, lures, and bait, as well as other outdoor supplies, such as golfing equipment. But there's a lot to do at the Bass Pro Shop other than buy. The store contains a four-story waterfall, a driving range and putting green, two restaurants, several well-stocked aquariums, and a wildlife museum filled with (stuffed) specimens of animals from around the world. The boating department resembles a boat show, with hundreds of models on display at every level of size and price. There are rifle and archery ranges where you can hone your skills at using the equipment you've just purchased. There's even a barber shop where you can have fishing lures made from locks of your newly shorn hair.

Obviously, creating, maintaining, and constantly updating a retail experience like this one is time-consuming and expensive. Does it pay off? Bass Pro Shops is the fastest-growing hunting and fishing supplier in the world. During 1998, over 4 million people visited the Springfield store, many for 2 days or more; many spent thousands of dollars during a single visit. Four new stores recently have been added to the Pro Shop chain—two in Florida, one each in Atlanta and Chicago—and six more are in the works.

The shopping experience also can be a powerful tool in the world of virtual business. Today's most successful e-tailers are turning the experience of shopping online into something unique and memorable. Consider eBay, the enormously popular Internet auction site. Hundreds of thousands of collectors shop eBay not only for the bargains they find but for the enormous communities of like-minded aficionados they meet. By providing a venue where fans of anything from Impressionist paintings to old movie posters to antique hand tools can gather and exchange ideas—as well as merchandise—eBay has developed an intensely loyal worldwide following (and become one of the few consistently profitable dotcom companies).

Retailers and e-tailers aren't the only ones who can use experience as a critical component of their business strategy. With imagination, companies in almost any business can develop this Core Competency in powerful, creative ways.

It starts with a commitment to transform the buying experience into a strategic asset. A bank that doesn't allow its best customers to stand in line, private lounges for retail clientele, personal shoppers who physically carry the goods back, a simple-to-navigate Web site that is intuitive to use and requires no transfer of credit-card information, e-mails confirming an order, confirming the shipping date, asking for confirmation of delivery, and feedback on use—all these are simple, cost-effective ways to use the experience of shopping with your brand to enhance its equity.

It is also possible to employ the Experience competency by transforming the experience of using and enjoying your product or service after the purchase has been made. Are you in the packaged goods business? Don't keep competing on price with yet another 20-cents-off coupon. Instead, look past the obvious for a broader, more creative definition of the experience associated with your product. It can be done with almost any product, not just those we naturally associate with exotic, dramatic, or emotional appeals.

Most packaged goods are consumed as part of some larger experience. Bacon, for example, is usually consumed with eggs, milk, bread, and coffee—at breakfast. You may not consider bacon very "experiential," like a pricey perfume or a box of gourmet chocolates (although customers who savor the smell of sizzling bacon on a chilly fall morning may disagree). But Sunday breakfast with the kids is a meaningful, enjoyable experience you can find ways to evoke on behalf of your brand. So is breakfast with Dad—or with a lover at a favorite country hideaway. These experiences offer a way to connect even humble product categories like bacon to another, more relevant event for the customer. Consider what Special K has done to associate its simple flakes with the experience of losing weight and looking and feeling physically fit—even sexy. Or Wheaties with champion athletes. Or Dr. Pepper with individualism.

If you can't afford to build such connections yourself, find other brands with whom you can strategically align yourself. For bacon, it could be a marketer of coffee, eggs, or juice—or, more adventurously, a travel agency or an airline ("Breakfast in Paris") or even a telephone company ("Share breakfast with Dad on Father's Day by calling long distance"). The only limitations are the nature of your brand's unique appeal and your own creativity.

The tactics, therefore, are simple. If your brand can deliver a unique experience in buying or consumption, consider it. If not, consider linking it with other important experiences that are memorable and easily associated with your brand.

Retailers, e-tailers, manufacturers, and service providers—all can make use of the Relationship strategy to reach and keep customers. The key is to begin thinking creatively about what you can do to make your Service and your customers' Experience with your brand unique, valuable, and memorable.

THE SECOND R: RETRENCHMENT

I have mentioned how the baby boomers in particular are beginning to withdraw from the traditional consumption environments. There are many reasons for this. In part, it's a natural result of aging; as people get older and less mobile, they devote less of their time to visiting malls and downtown shopping areas. They need less—but they want more. Trends in the economy of the 1990s are factors, too. Working people are more pressed for time than ever, making buying less of an enjoyable diversion and more of an unpleasant necessity to be finished as efficiently and quickly as possible. And in truth, it's partly our fault. Frankly, we've often failed to give most customers much of a reason to leave their homes to buy our products and services.

Retrenchment is a strategy for dealing with this problem in the New Economy. It involves *going to the customer* rather than trying to entice him or her to come to us. There are two Core Competencies that can be used to support a Retrenchment strategy—*Technology* and *Convenience*.

Technology

One Retrenchment technique is to use Technology to bring the store, the brand, or the service into the customer's home or office. The great direct-mail retailers have done this for years—Lands' End, L.L. Bean, Lillian Vernon, and many others. Today's newest technologies are adding a new wrinkle to this business approach. E-tailers are building a competitive advantage by using the Internet and other electronic systems to reach customers instantly.

Not every business category has yet been colonized successfully by the e-tailers, although almost every one has been tried. Books, music, travel, and technology products (software, computers, electronic gadgets) have led the way in Internet commerce for several interesting and revealing reasons. First, these are business categories of special interest to young, well-educated, affluent consumers. Of course, these are the kinds of people currently most likely to be surfing the net, but they also represent the leading edge for the Next Economy. It's easy to conclude that as these youthful consumers broaden their interests in the years to come, almost every type of product and service will take up residence on the Internet. Billions in revenues are waiting for the entrepreneurs who grab the new businesses that emerge—using Next Economy practices.

Second, the current hot e-tailing businesses are ones in which customers, especially baby boomers, are used to buying without extensive hands-on inspection of the goods. (Book and music lovers like to browse the aisles of their favorite stores, true, but they generally buy based mainly on the identity of the title and artist they want.) Thus the degree of interactivity currently possible on the net is sufficient to let customers feel comfortable with buying electronically those brands and products with which they are familiar.

It probably will take a couple of more years to perfect the technology needed to facilitate buying fashion (for example) over the Internet. But it's coming. Voyant Corporation, for example, has already created technology that allows customers to take an eye test online, generates the reading-glasses strength you need, and then captures your image and allows you to see yourself in one of 15,000 frame styles. An image-manipulation program known as Zoom allows Internet users to study product pictures in close-up—for example, to narrowly examine the weave of the denim in a pair of jeans—with a few clicks of the mouse. The Lands' End Web site currently features a computer program that makes it possible to see your own image "trying on" many different sportswear outfits. At other sites, you can see your room decorated with a selection of alternative rugs and window treatments. More improvements in what you can see, hear, and even feel on the Internet are sure to come.

Also note that the business categories currently most popular on the Web—books, music, travel, and technology—are now among the most deflationary. In all four categories, downward price pressure is intense for several reasons but especially because of the trend toward rapid obsolescence of inventory. Thus it makes sense for manufacturers, retailers, and distributors in these fields to, in effect, merge, customizing products as they are ordered and shipping them out fast rather than maintaining a warehouse full of inventory losing its value daily. As I have mentioned, Dell and Gateway, among others, have built fabulously successful computer businesses on this strategy—product manufacturers who have made themselves into great consumer brand names by using technology to support a retrenchment strategy. Others almost certainly will follow suit in brown goods—home theater and customized audio systems, for example.

A carefully plotted retrenchment strategy can have other advantages. Book and music e-tailers such as Amazon, which have generally maintained small inventories of product and ordered goods as needed from wholesalers and publishers, have had an inherent advantage over traditional companies that maintain warehouses holding thousands of copies of today's—and yesterday's—would-be best-sellers. Of course, Amazon has yet to turn a profit, despite this cost advantage. It remains to be seen how Amazon will fare now that it has built a network of warehouses, thereby sacrificing one of the distinctions that formerly made it unique. In its place is a focus on using technology for personalized service. This transition is perhaps the most important and potentially profitable change in priority Amazon has yet implemented.

It is not economies of scale or cost-out accounting that is driving Retrenchment. It is the fact that customers are *demanding* it. Retrenchment comes at a time when Mom is better educated and smarter about buying than ever. She doesn't need merchants to decide what products she should choose from; she knows what she wants. And technology has given her the opportunity to exercise her newly found consuming power. As a result, marketing is shifting from a push-dominated process, moving products and services from manufacturers to customers, to a pull-dominated one, where the customer demands and everyone else reacts, with Retrenchment as a natural outgrowth. New marketing solutions are essential to make Technology a servant of profitability rather than a drain on it.

Convenience

At the turn of the last century, the great Sears, Roebuck catalogue was the universal wish list of American consumers, a business built around the latest technologies of that day: rapid, nationwide postal service and freight delivery by train and truck. In Canada, it was the Eatons Book. The same model has been used successfully right into our own time. It's at the heart of the second form of Retrenchment strategy: to differentiate your brand by offering Convenience. It differs from Technology in that it uses old distribution and communication systems rather than new technology to deliver the product or service. At its base, however, it too is about selling Mom in her environment rather than coaxing her out into yours.

As the baby-boom cohort marches through middle age, more and more smart businesses are deploying Convenience as a key part of their marketing strategy. The TV-based retailing networks—QVC, the Home Shopping Network, and The Shopping Channel (in Canada)—are one example of how this can be done. Another is the proliferation of 1-800 numbers for telephone ordering of products, ranging from flowers to mattresses to theater tickets. Still another is the new shop-at-home health care services, which can deliver goods such as pharmaceutical products and contact lenses to your front door. In an increasingly elderly America, this Core Competency is likely to become more, not less, important as the Next Economy engulfs us.

Up to now, Convenience has not been easy for consumer-goods manufacturers to adopt because it involves bypassing their existing retail infrastructure. As we've seen, most retailers make a significant portion of their bottom line on rebates, display allowances, and other fees from the manufacturing segment—that is, they make money on their buying, not their selling. Naturally, then, they are reluctant to allow their vendors to talk directly to their customers and so bypass them. But all this is changing. Authors are publishing their books online, bypassing the traditional book retailers. Composers and bands are creating music for sale online. Personal services in travel, finance, and other areas are being developed specifically for online customers.

Long-cycle, thoughtfully considered purchases such as automobiles, expensive stereos, and upscale home furnishings probably will be among the first to move to this Convenience option. They'll soon be followed by new packaged goods companies that lack the long-standing business obligations that restrict established brands. Eventually, virtually every business segment will include companies that have found ways to make Convenience into a unique competitive advantage. Most retailers won't like this, but it's inevitable. For many non-B2C compa-nies, Convenience is an excuse to manage all points of customer con-tact, including communicating and marketing directly to the customers' customers.

As a strategist, I must warn you that there's an inherent weakness in the Retrenchment strategy. Businesses built around either Technology or Convenience often lack personal contact, something for which we humans have an innate craving. I can't imagine a world in which most people are content to remain at home, forgoing human interaction in favor of consuming, learning, communicating, and living electronically. And while I can speak metaphorically of having a relationship with a product—a favorite cereal or a pair of jeans—it's not the same as con-necting in the flesh with a person or people who embody a brand. This is exactly why the Web-centric companies in the New Economy failed and the Next Economy will need human contact to succeed.

For this reason, a state-of-the-art customer-care center will be a prerequisite for success for those using Retrenchment strategies. The call centers of the Old and New Economies were largely reactive. The call center of the Next Economy will be proactive. Those who staff it will represent the customer within your corporation. They'll be increasingly responsible for massaging the relationship between your brand and your customers—particularly if you use Technology or Con-venience as your Core Competency.

THE THIRD R: RELEVANCY

Throughout this book, I have talked about the importance of becoming relevant to your best customers. Some people may believe that Rele-vancy is more important than Retrenchment, Rewards, or Relation-ships. I believe that most successful Next Economy companies will need at least one dimension of relevance as a pillar of their strategy because the contact points are so intense for the customer.

Relevancy is a critical strategy in the Next Economy because busi-nesses will be competing primarily in the Q_2 and Q_3 segments, where some loyalty exists but customers are still vulnerable to competitive offerings. The objective of a relevancy strategy is to tie your brand's equity directly to the dominant purchase motivators for the category. You can do this best through *Expertise* or *Merchandising*.

Expertise

The first Core Competency associated with this strategy is Expertise: making your company the number one source of ideas and information about the category within which you compete. Almost all specialty retailers use this method, as do many companies in the service businesses. And as you'll see, some of the smartest packaged-goods and consumer-products manufacturers also have had success with the Expertise strategy.

A good example of a company that has used the Expertise competency in building brand equity is Radio Shack. This company has carefully developed and nurtured an image as the most knowledgeable and accessible source of information for the home electronics buff or hobbyist. Home Depot is another example. It hired experienced professionals from the various contracting crafts (plumbers, electricians, and the like) to advise customers in their areas of expertise. Thus, if you're buying lumber to enlarge your back yard deck, Home Depot will make sure you talk to a retired carpenter who can tell you the right size of galvanized nails to use and what time of year is best to apply a water-resistant finish.

Yet another example is the PetsMart superstore chain, which caters to animal lovers and pet owners of all kinds. Each of the sales associates at PetsMart is a trained expert on choosing and caring for a particular category of pet; if you need advice on what to feed a parrot, for example, you can seek out a sales associate wearing a button with the image of a bird, knowing that this means that he or she has been specially trained to help with bird-related questions.

Expertise needn't be provided by salespeople. (In this sense, it differs from the related Core Competency of Service. Service is almost always people-based; Expertise is knowledge-based and can be conveyed in any convenient and helpful way, whether through people or not.) A customer-care center can be a source of Expertise; so can an online information service preloaded with answers to 200 frequently asked questions (FAQs); and so can a book, brochure, or CD published with your company's imprimatur that offers unique and valuable ideas about home repair, entertainment, personal finance—whatever your field of specialization happens to be.

With a little ingenuity, almost any business can use Expertise as a differentiating factor. The most popular veterinarian in Armonk, New York, attained that status largely because of a series of clear, simple, up-to-date one-page flyers she wrote that explain to pet owners every-thing they need to know about a particular animal health problem. If you learn that your dog has a case of Lyme disease, Dr. Padilla will not only answer all your questions but also will supply you with a flyer sum-marizing the answers and making special recommendations about care and treatment tailored to the climate and conditions of suburban Armonk. This is Expertise in action on a small but very effective scale.

Expertise is becoming a huge issue in e-commerce. The most popu-lar and effective selling sites on the Web—perhaps ironically—are those which provide definitive, *non-sales-oriented* Expertise in particular subject areas. Amazon, the book and music e-tailer, is an example. It grew rapidly in the middle to late 1990s by avoiding the temptation to ply visitors with ads and pitches for the books and CDs it (or the pub-lishers) wanted to sell. Instead, at your option, the company would list for you the latest books and CDs you're likely to enjoy, based on a com-parison of your past buying patterns with the books and CDs other cus-tomers have bought. A reader of Civil War history books might be offered *Cold Mountain*, a novel with a Civil War background; a lover of Dorothy Sayers's mystery novels might be introduced to the thrillers of Margery Allingham.

The key for any e-commerce success is for the Web site to meet the customer's wants by whisking her through the site as quickly, easily, and entertainingly as possible, giving her access to its unique Expertise in a painless, enjoyable fashion. This is the kind of experience that will draw customers back to the same site frequently—and produce sales.

Expertise can be used successfully by companies offering packaged goods and other consumer products as well. Kraft arguably built its dominant share in packaged cheeses and related foods using advertising built around "hands and recipes," demonstrations of easy, creative, and delicious ways to use Kraft products in family meals. Kraft also was among the first businesses to link its ad budget to direct-response mechanisms through mail-in recipe offers and later through 800 num-bers offering tips for product preparation and serving.

Another example is Shell Oil's creation of a powerful image of Expertise in auto maintenance and highway safety through the publi-cation of a host of popular and truly useful booklets filled with infor-mation on everything from improving your car's gas mileage to avoiding flat tires. Shell separated itself from its competitors in an otherwise undistinguished marketplace by an Expertise strategy that made consumers think of their local Shell station as the best source for informed and caring help with their cars. Interestingly, Mobil opted to position itself in the New Economy not on Expertise but on Technology and Rewards by focusing on their high-speed transactional wand that whisks you through the payment process in moments. Shell and Mobil are two supposed brands competing in a commodity market with very separate and distinguishable strategies—both operating under the Four R umbrella, both highly probable successes in the New Economy, but built on different customer contact points.

Merchandise

Another way of achieving Relevancy is through a unique mix of Merchandise. By offering products or services that are carefully and intelligently selected to cater specifically to the wants of your Q_1 and Q_2 customers, your Merchandise choices can make you, in effect, the number one procurement manager for your customers—the supplier they trust to make a smart first cut at what they'll be buying.

Merchandise is another critical customer contact point. What you sell and how you display it is what makes you a destination banner. What you make and how you package it makes you a destination brand. What you make and how you service it makes you a destination vendor.

Merchandise as a Core Competency must fall under the control of marketing if it is to be used as a strategic point of differentiation. In the Old Economy, merchandising and buying in the retail and e-tail space fell to separate organizations within the company, not to marketing. Likewise in packaged goods and services, product-development specialists, quality-control people, engineers, and scientists developed and managed the physical product line. Marketing usually was left with the job of supporting these products or services once management approved them.

In the Next Economy, merchandising and product development must come under the direct management of marketing people. If the concept of marketing is to succeed, it must represent Q_1 and Q_2 customers' wants in the product mix the company offers. This cannot be left to people who have no day-to-day contact with the customer base.

Having buyers who meet with vendors to collaborate on what merchandise will be available allows almost no customer input whatsoever. It can't possibly work in the Next Economy, where intimate knowledge of customer wants is the key to building profitable brand equity—where consistency in managing all customer contact points by definition must include the customers' contact with the product or service.

Fashion marketers, for example, have to decide whether they are an *item house* or a *look house*. This is Merchandise strategy. An item house displays and sells one item at a time—one stock keeping unit (SKU). It may be a blouse, a purse, or a pair of shoes. The items are organized by item, department, and category. By contrast, a look house displays and sells an outfit, a look—and, by extension, a lifestyle, a feeling. When the display includes not only the blouse but the skirt, shoes, bag, hat, and scarf that go beautifully with it, you make it easy for the customer to buy more. This is one of the simple success secrets of The Gap. Customers can't go wrong buying fashion at The Gap, Old Navy, or Banana Republic because, for each season, entire ensembles are pulled together in colors, fabrics, and looks that match perfectly. The brand's relevancy is contained in the very selection of products found on the floor and how they're displayed.

More and more intelligent retailers are beginning to apply the look-house approach to marketing areas other than apparel. Visit a Pottery Barn retail store, for example, and notice how its table fashion displays are coordinated. Why can't other types of retailers do the same? In a hardware store, why not display together all the tools, equipment, and supplies needed to build a garden trellis or some other favorite project, along with instructional books and videos to explain how?

For packaged-goods brands, the real conflict is between intelligent broadening of the brands' product line and extending it into unrelated or marginally related areas. Smart Merchandise choices for manufacturers involve applying your brand names consistently and avoiding the temptation to stretch them beyond where they holistically belong. For decades, the Campbell's brand drove the ready-made soup business because the quality of its line, the consistency of its packaging, and its refusal to water down what "Campbell's" meant built credibility on the store shelf. In fact, great consumer companies like Campbell's, Tropicana, Heinz, Coca-Cola, Budweiser, and almost every other leading brand built their equity on "narrow and deep" branding rather than "wide and shallow" branding.

Trouble begins when you allow your brands to be extended haphazardly into unrelated or marginally related product categories. New flavors of Dannon yogurt—of course. Dannon frozen yogurt pops—okay. But Dannon spring water? The connection seems to be a tenuous one. One or two more "stretches" like this recent new product introduction and the Dannon brand name may come to lose its meaning—and once that's gone, it takes a long, long time to build it up again. Smart marketers are cautious about brand extensions—and they don't allow product managers to "borrow" another brand's equity, using it to expand into new product categories just because they don't have the money to build a second brand.

As you've probably noticed, the underlying strength of all successful Merchandise approaches is *focus*—a clear-eyed understanding of the target customer and a selection of products or services that meet his or her needs precisely. The corresponding cardinal sin is lack of focus—stretching your offerings to include merchandise or categories that destroy any coherent image for your brand or banner and make no sense to the customer.

A classic example of how stretching a brand name through illogical Merchandise selection can trash brand equity involves a home electronics retailer I once advised. Nobody Beats The Wiz had grown to be the preeminent purveyor of stereos, TVs, and other home electronics in the Northeast, thanks largely to the careful nurturing of an image as the retailer with the best selection of top-name electronics merchandise at reasonable prices. Nonetheless, I could never convince the management of Nobody Beats The Wiz to change one merchandise choice that did almost as much to shatter that image as its expensive TV and radio advertising campaigns did to build it. The old management insisted on selling watches and sunglasses, which, to the average consumer, have no natural connection to expensive home electronics and entertainment gear. Worse, management displayed this merchandise in the most important, high-traffic part of each Nobody Beats The Wiz store—within 50 feet of the entrance. Shoppers, confused and disappointed by the displays that greeted them inside the doors, had a lot to overcome before they ever reached the attractive rooms filled with big-screen TVs and CD players that were the store's real purpose and focus.

The old management team never understood this, which contributed to its failure several years ago. In its wake is a new management team at what is now called simply The Wiz. The new team has converted the front-of-store space to incorporate displays of high-technology electronic toys and gadgets similar to what you might see in a Sharper Image store or catalog. This is much more compatible with the "entertainment" positioning that these managers have defined for the company and its focus on Expertise.

In the Next Economy, Merchandise replaces the old P, product, from the Old Economy. The ability of product-development departments and retail buyers to empathize with their Q_1 and Q_2 customers will be the key to a successful Merchandise strategy. Merchandise can be relevant only if it reflects what your best customers want. And unless your people spend as much time with your customers as they spend with your vendors in the laboratory, they cannot hope to succeed in the demand-driven Next Economy.

THE FOURTH R: REWARDS

Just as the name suggests, this fourth R—*Rewards*—defines strategies built around rewarding consumers for doing business with you. There are, again, two Core Competencies you can employ in carrying out a rewards strategy: *Stature* and *Time*.

Stature

Certain brands and stores are so respected that simply being a customer of theirs carries an intrinsic psychological reward. Think about how much delight people get out of giving a gift of jewelry that comes in a box of a particular shade of pale blue. (You can picture it instantly, can't you?) That's stature. It's the pleasure customers get from being associated with a particular brand or banner—as if the brand equity rubs off on the customer, adding luster and enjoyment to his or her life.

The great upscale retailers, from Tiffany and Nordstrom to Bloomingdales and Harrod's, all offer stature as one of the benefits of shopping with them. Stature is also a significant component of brand value in many packaged goods and other consumer products. Just think Kraft cheeses versus any supermarket's private-label competitor, Donna Karan versus any department-store brand of women's sportswear, Mercedes versus Hyundai, Rolex versus Timex. And the same applies to service businesses: I believe that a Cunard cruise, a dinner at Le Cirque, and a hairstyling by Vidal Sassoon offer more Stature than the corresponding services from Carnival Cruises, the Olive Garden, or Joan's neighborhood salon. (Those lower-Stature brands, of course, may have other strengths on which their Equity is based.)

In the shop-till-you-drop 1980s, Stature usually meant upscale. You remember the brand names of that era and the icons that went with them, some of which are still popular today: the initials LV on a dark brown handbag, a little alligator on the breast of a knitted shirt, the acronym BMW on a German car.

In today's more complicated marketing environment, stature itself has become more complicated. Upscale is still powerful, and probably always will be—at least as long as wealth retains its allure. In the 1990s, however, and into the next millennium, it's cool in many circles to brag about how *little* you pay for the goods and services you enjoy. This is part of the appeal of the flea market, the out-of-the-way art gallery, or the antiques shop at the end of a dusty country road: The items we buy there don't come adorned with designer logos, but when we find a treasure that we can buy for a fraction of its value, we love to display it in our home and brag about what a steal it was. That, too, is Stature.

Every subgroup in our society has its own special flavor of Stature. Among teenagers, Stature adheres to the latest hot pop group, movie, TV show, or sports team; predicting where Stature will stick next in the youth culture is almost impossible (although fortunes have been made and lost based on it).

Among those fascinated by technology, there's Stature in whatever is newest, most powerful, most complex, like the latest audio and video gear.

What's the moral? Know your best customers. Get under the skin of your Q_1 and Q_2 customers and learn what they value most: Is it prestige, modernity, cheap chic, machismo, exoticism, sophistication, simplicity? Once you know, look for every opportunity to associate your brand or banner with that quality until your logo becomes an icon that immediately evokes a particular lifestyle and personality with which one profitable swath of customers is eager to be associated.

Time

As an aspect of the Rewards strategy, Time doesn't necessarily refer to convenience (although, in today's high-pressure world, most of us are usually seeking ways to save rather than to spend time). It refers, rather, to the investment of time in the acquisition and use of the product or service you are offering. Whenever your brand is linked to an especially rewarding, valuable, enjoyable, or effective use of time, you can be said to be pursuing a Time strategy.

The simplest and most obvious form of Time strategy is, in fact, saving time for your customers. The reason that Time will become a strategic building block in the Next Economy is because, for many people, it is a scarcer resource than money. Time is finite. You can't borrow it. You can't lend it. As a result, its value to customers is continually increasing.

The Time strategy has many variations:

- *Get me in and out quickly*—as used by McDonalds and other fast-food stores, drive-through bank windows, express lanes in supermarkets, pay-at-the-pump gas stations, and so on.
- *Bring the product or service to me*—as used by any and all home-delivery services (for fresh or prepared food, dry cleaning, newspapers, what have you) or by any at-home service supplier (from teachers and tutors to masseurs, trainers, and therapists).
- *Move the store to my block*—as used by banks with hundreds of ATM locations, vending machines selling everything from sodas and candy to newspapers and sandwiches, and kiosks for photo developing.
- *Put it all under one roof*—as when Kinko's, the photo copy shop, offers a range of small business services in each location, including office supplies, computer rentals, and overnight express delivery.

In many packaged-goods and consumer-products categories, Time is a critical differentiating factor and equity builder. The entire frozen-food category was invented to take advantage of Time as a customer benefit. So were a host of other food products:

- "Brown and serve" dishes that go from freezer to oven to table in 30 minutes or less
- Prepared meals including center plate plus veggies and dessert in a single package, à la Healthy Choice
- Pregrated cheese for home-made pizza, prewashed salad greens, precut deli meats

And the same logic underlies many nonfood products: preshrunk jeans, condensed books, water-soluble paints, and others. These are all time-saving strategies.

The other main Time strategy involves turning the time spent acquiring your product or service into a pleasurable or valuable interlude—an investment in time that the customer cherishes rather than resents. At different moments in life, we all appreciate both kinds of Time strategies.

When we're working on deadline, we like grabbing a drive-through lunch at Taco Bell; when we're celebrating a wedding anniversary, we appreciate a 4-hour, multicourse dinner in a romantic setting (and we'll gladly pay for the time it takes). When we're shopping for tonight's groceries, we'll use the express line at the A&P; when we're spending an unexpected end-of-year bonus on some special holiday gifts for the ones we love, we relish an afternoon with a personal shopper at Bloomingdale's. When we're leaving for a business trip on tonight's redeye, we value a hairdresser who'll come to our office to give us a quick trim while we work; when we have a long weekend off, we cherish a day of pampering at the beauty spa.

Associating your brand with moments of pleasure places it in a new context. In this context, time is not saved but savored. For many companies providing commoditized goods or services, this association can help you build brand value in a powerful way.

Consider the great current DeBeers diamond marketing campaign, which places the gift of a diamond in the context of a supremely romantic moment: a dance on a moonlit balcony or an embrace on a sunlit beach. In fact, a diamond is a literal commodity, bearing no identifying mark or logo and sold according to weight and other technical specifications. However, by associating the diamond with a cherished moment in time, DeBeers lifts the product out of the category of a commodity and vastly increases its brand equity in the customer's mind.

THE MARKETER MUST CHOOSE

As I've outlined the Four R's—these new tools for the modern marketing toolbox—you've probably noticed how varied they are. Equally varied are the companies I've cited as successful exemplars of the use of the Four R's—from upscale brands like Nordstrom and Tiffany to mass-market ones like Taco Bell and J.C. Penney. I have cited retailers ranging from

Bloomingdale's to PetsMart to your favorite flea market and e-tailers from Amazon and Dell to eBay and Landsend.com. I have talked about great consumer product brands, from Rolex and Campbell's to Mercedes and Kraft, and I have praised service providers from Kinko's copy shops and Cunard cruises to Vidal Sassoon and even a local veterinarian. What's the common thread that unites them all?

Answer: *They've all made clear, sharp, intelligent choices of marketing strategies from among the Four R's and the Eight Core Competencies.* As a result, each has a distinctive marketing style aimed at a specific target customer whose business and loyalty are worth attracting and keeping.

Whether they realize it or not, all the most successful businesses of today and tomorrow are already using brand-equity strategies based on some combination of the Four R's and the Eight Core Competencies associated with them.

The unique "footprint" of any business is determined by the choices it makes among these strategic elements. If you are a visual thinker, you can plot the Four R's and the Eight Core Competencies onto a matrix, as shown in Figure 8-1. By executing both management and customer research, you can determine the relative importance of these competencies to your business and then plot them onto the matrix, as shown in Figures 8-2 through 8-4.

You can see how different the footprints are, depending on the type of business-to-customer (B2C) business you operate. A convenience store's mission-critical competencies are in convenience and transactional time. This looks and is very different from a category killer such as PetsMart, where merchandise and expertise drive the business. And PetsMart's Core Competencies are shaped very differently from those of a full-service department store such as Macy's, where the brands it sells, coupled with the merchandise and service, drive the category.

Once the strategy is defined, building a vision statement and writing the process to institutionalize the Core Competencies can be done. But companies that refuse to discipline themselves or that choose among the eight competencies haphazardly, without considering the unique requirements of their best customers, are almost certain to fail.

Managing the Four R's and the Eight Core Competencies is a prerequisite for anyone trying to develop an intelligent marketing plan for the new millennium because they in turn give you control over all the customer contact points. They don't represent the *one* smart marketing strategy you must follow today—*there is no such strategy.* Instead, they

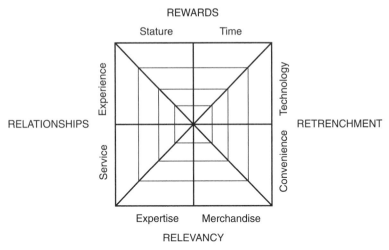

Figure 8-1 The Four R's equity matrix.

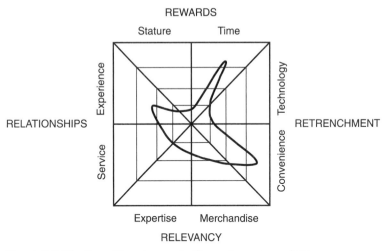

Figure 8-2 The Four R's equity matrix: Convenience store—7-11.

represent the blend of alternatives you have to choose from. Think of them as the ingredients for a spaghetti sauce. Most sauces use the same basic ingredients—tomatoes, garlic, cheese, herbs, spices—but each has a unique taste because of its special blending of those ingredients.

Finally, please remember that in the coming deflationary environment, where the total market for most products and services is shrinking, success will not be measured by same-day sales, last year's sales to date

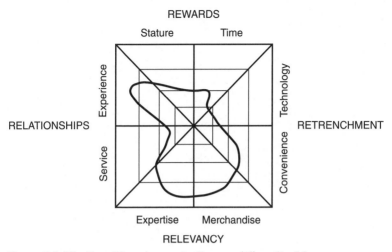

Figure 8-3 The Four R's equity matrix: Category killer—PetsMart.

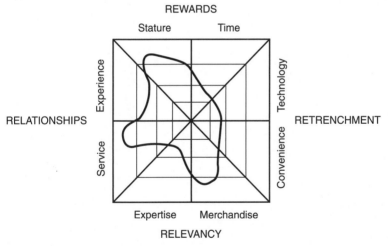

Figure 8-4 The Four R's equity matrix: Department store—Macy's.

versus this year's sales to date, or other traditional metrics. Success will be about *profits*. The Next Economy is all about enhancing the value of your brand with your best customers by using your knowledge of what they want to build a more meaningful relationship with them—one that consistently delights them at every point of contact. The Four R's and the Eight Core Competencies are the best way I know to get there.

9

Tools, Techniques, and Structures for Comarketing

As you can clearly tell, the battle of the Next Economy will not be for awareness or share of market. It will be for relevancy and share of best-customer spending. Those brands which build their equity based on values that their want segments best relate to will capture a higher degree of relevancy with the Q_1 and Q_2 target.

Not all brands are in fact very relevant to most people. As we've seen, the brands that matter to people are those with which they share a value structure. In most cases, however, the brand relationship is a minuscule part of the customer's life. In these cases, it may be difficult to try to apply the Next Economy methods directly. The relationship between the customer and the brand is too infrequent or produces too little annualized gross profit to allow you to invest enough money in building a meaningful relationship alone.

Remember, marketers spend (or should spend) 100 percent of their time thinking about their customers. But customers spend only a small fraction of their time thinking about the brand.

Comarketing offers a solution to this dilemma.

CUSTOMER INVOLVEMENT

One way to think about this is in terms of the *customer-involvement spectrum*. Every product has a certain level of involvement associated with it, based on a series of factors. In part, customer involvement is based on purchase frequency. The more often you buy something, the less risk there is, because you'll soon have another opportunity to change brands. Involvement is also a function of the cost of the product in comparison with the total you expect to spend in the entire category. The higher the cost, the more attention customers pay to the company and brand and the greater the involvement.

Whether the product is used socially or personally also affects its involvement level. Socially used products are badges of status and values because your use of them is public. Cars, appliances, clothing, and almost anything that communicates your values, tastes, or attitudes are badge products. Badge products generally carry a high involvement value because you are making a statement about yourself that others can read, so customer involvement in such categories tends to be quite high.

Likewise, personal-care products have high involvement values. These include cosmetics, health and beauty aids, eye-care products, etc. These categories carry high involvement levels because they are very personal decisions and because many offer little ways of rewarding and spoiling ourselves. It is the personal nature of the category that drives its involvement with the customer.

High rates of technological change also drive up a category's involvement level. This is so because these changes make products obsolete more quickly than most. Thus the involvement is driven by a need for knowledge about how quickly the product or service will become obsolete.

Today, for example, high-definition TV (HDTV) has a very high involvement level, which is why it has taken so long to get traction in the marketplace. Q_1 and Q_2 customers who normally might have the desire and the means to purchase these new "toys" have stayed away because the technology is in flux and the programming is still not broadly available. Even though the transaction hasn't taken place, the product category still has a large involvement level.

The consumption model also drives involvement higher. In every act of consumption, there can be a purchaser, a user, an influencer, and a decision maker. It is possible to have as many as four or five people affected by the transaction or as few as one (if a single person plays all the roles). The cereal Mom buys is influenced by the children, consumed by Dad as well as the kids, purchased by Mom, and chosen by Mom. It's an inexpensive product with a high involvement level. At the opposite end of the spectrum might be a ballpoint pen or a candy bar. These, like many products and services, carry a low involvement level in part because only one person is involved in the transaction/consumption model. This is why low-involvement products are often impulse buys, generated at the store or Web site.

You can see that high-involvement categories of products and services lend themselves to branding. Remember, the effectiveness of branding is always based on relevance, and in a high-involvement category, the purchase decision is by definition a highly relevant one for the customer. When you buy a low-involvement item such as a roll of toilet paper, you may devote 5 seconds to the decision, and you may not even notice what brand you buy. When you buy a high-involvement item such as a new car, the decision may take months, and brand values certainly will play a major role. Not coincidentally, low-involvement products are often more need-based, while high-involvement products are more want-based.

Businesses whose products and services are in high-involvement categories are lucky because, for them, most of the Next Economy strategies are feasible. Brands in the low-involvement categories face a very different challenge. For companies that own them, this chapter may be the most important in this book.

Sometimes it's possible to move a product, through clever positioning, from the low-involvement category to a higher-involvement category. Many years ago, I worked with Papermate Pens to develop a relevance strategy for its brand. A pen is normally a low-involvement purchase. (The one exception would be a fine pen being purchased as a gift, which is high-involvement and high-relevancy.) Many people don't even buy pens—they just "borrow" them from their workplaces. Thus most people don't draw strong distinctions among pen brands—Papermate, Bic, Pentel, Parker, and so on. The challenge we faced: How to make the Papermate brand more relevant to more people?

The solution we came up with was this: To build the sense of relevance and involvement for the category (and the brand), we talked in our advertising about what happens when you buy a *bad* pen. We showed people smudging the signature on an important contract; we showed a cheap pen leaking ink all over someone's tuxedo jacket; we showed someone pulling out a pen to sign the check in a fancy restaurant and having it dribble ink on them. We had to create a new sense of involvement for the category, thereby increasing the relevance of the decision in the customer's mind.

This kind of strategy sometimes can be used for low-involvement products. For most businesses in low-relevance categories, however, there are two effective ways to go in the Next Economy:

- Use sponsorship to associate yourself with other things that *are* important to customers.
- Comarket with a number of other brands, thereby creating a pooled sense of relevance.

Both strategies can move your brand from low relevancy to significant degrees of involvement. In this chapter we'll consider the pros, cons, and implications of both in the Next Economy.

SPONSORSHIP MARKETING

In sponsorship marketing, you are strategically associating your brand with something important to the customer—an activity, a belief, a cause, a passion. The objective is to link your brand to more relevant issues in your customers' lives in order to increase the involvement level.

Consider, for example, the fact that Tide detergent is a cosponsor of Nascar auto racing. Some users are very brand loyal when buying laundry detergent. For others, it is a commoditized product, habitually purchased with a low involvement level. Linking Tide to Nascar associates the brand with a positive experience about which millions of auto racing fans feel passionately. The sponsorship also lets Procter & Gamble run a series of spin-off activities. Tide customers can collect purchase points with which to get such Nascar memorabilia as autographed photos of top drivers; Tide can arrange to have a snazzy racing car (emblazoned with Tide logos, of course) displayed at shopping centers. All of this ups the involvement level for Tide well beyond normal.

Similar effects can be produced through many kinds of sponsoring. Depending on the size of the company and its marketing budgets, a brand could sponsor such activities as a swim meet, a stamp collectors' convention, the Olympic Games, a state rodeo, or a 10K charity run for cancer prevention. A natural connection between the brand and the sponsored activity is not essential. The message is: We recognize that our best customers (those in Q_1 and Q_2) are passionate about this activity, so we support it. The implication is: We share your values. You share our brand.

The case of Tide sponsoring Nascar is an interesting one because laundry detergent is a "female" product, whereas auto racing is usually perceived as a "male" interest. However, the fact is that Nascar is a hugely popular phenomenon around the United States, with millions of women fans. Furthermore, Procter & Gamble derives ancillary benefits from the sponsorship in terms of its relationship with "the trade," that is, the distributors of products to grocery stores. Most of the people working in the trade are male, and they get a kick out of going to events like Nascar races with their families and taking home the "tchatchkes"— caps, bags, jackets—from the Tide-sponsored tent or booth.

The sponsorship relationship is clearly working for Tide. It's also working for other "female" product categories with low involvement levels: Cheerios, Kellogg's, and K-Mart are also Nascar sponsors.

If the fit between brand and sponsored event is a natural one, it's even better. Thus, when cosmetics companies sponsor events related to women's health issues, as Revlon does with breast cancer research, the logic of the association is strong. In this case, involvement levels can be driven way up the scale through the brand's association with a cause that is critical to Q_1 and Q_2 customers.

HORIZONTAL COMARKETING

Comarketing traditionally has been hosted in the vertical space between retailers and vendors or distributors or on Web pages—in other words, in collaboration with the companies ahead of you or behind you in the supply chain. You're probably familiar with the many retail vendor programs, often called *co-op programs*, that are all vertical programs in this sense—for example, when Campbell's soup is highlighted on a flyer from A&P or Kroger's. The brand shares its equity with the banner (the retail brand), and together they make a proposition to the customer.

In the Next Economy, however, *horizontal comarketing* will be the big new trend. Here, the idea is to share your Q_1 and Q_2 customers with other companies—companies with whom you may have nothing important in common *except* customers. Your goal is to add relevance and involvement to the purchase of your product by amalgamating the buying power of a basket of brands that share many of the same Q_1 and Q_2 customers. Individually, these brands may not command much of your customers' mindshare; together, they represent a significant issue.

In concrete terms, this kind of comarketing often can be done through a point-accumulation strategy. Five or six brands can be bundled together to create cumulative buying power and to reward the customer appropriately for given levels of purchasing.

In setting up a horizontal comarketing program, you'll be looking for companies with customers who are buying heavily in several categories that don't compete with yours. Marketers could marry Kraft cheeses with Quaker Oats cereals, Oscar Meyer bacon, and Dannon yogurt, combining them in a basket of products that share nothing except a customer in common.

Some horizontal comarketing programs are built around natural themes. Thus, when barbecue season arrives, it's not unusual for a collection of companies that sell bread, hot dogs, barbecue sauce, and charcoal briquettes to get together and build a cobranding concept focused on an event (backyard cooking) and a particular customer (the woman who buys all these things). The customer might get a free set of barbecue accessories if she buys all four products. Or she might go into her favorite store and find a large display with a barbecue banner and all four products on display. Or she might receive a comprehensive barbecue recipe book as a reward for buying all four products.

As you can see, the idea is to become significant enough in the customer's mind to build a relationship with her—at least for the basket of brands that includes yours. An event like our hypothetical barbecue event could become an annual program. As you know, Memorial Day, Father's Day, Independence Day, and Labor Day are the crucial holiday weekends for barbecuing. A strategic alliance such as the one I've described here could help participating marketers capture the lion's share of business on these weekends. The result: It's a lot easier to make your annual budget, and more important, over time the emotions attached to these weekends get attached to your brand.

Such a horizontal comarketing program could be carried to the next highest level by finding the households that have large numbers of children or the strongest neighborhood ties. These are the households most likely to buy large quantities of barbecue products. How can you find them? In the Old Economy, it couldn't be done at a reasonable cost. In the Next Economy, new techniques make it feasible. Customers will be encouraged to log onto a Web site where they can punch in the UPC numbers from their latest purchase. The site will then ask a few questions about the customer's consumption pattern. (Obviously, a worthwhile inducement will have to be offered—a special gift, prize, or other reward.) This information will give the company a good feel for what quintile the customer falls into. From this beachhead, a narrow and more relevant marketing program could be developed—one that is relevant to summer barbecue customers all the other weeks of the year. The company that makes barbecue sauce, for example, could provide mustard recipes at Thanksgiving.

Many companies already use this method to cross-promote their own products and brands. This is usually a mistake. It's based on the somewhat arrogant assumption that your brand names and your products are similarly important to the Q_1 and Q_2 customers. This *may* be true, but it's unlikely. Instead of assuming this to be the case, design your program starting with what's best for the customer. Give your customer the opportunity to buy her favorite brands in all the relevant product categories *across* companies.

Look at the relatively new relationship between Amazon.com and Toys R Us. Amazon will now host the Toys R Us Web site and handle the distribution. Originally driven by the need to marry the expertise of each company, this comarketing effort is likely to succeed not because of the cost savings it will generate but because the involvement level for both brands will move up as the Amazon site becomes as synonymous with toys as it already is for books.

Using the Toys R Us brand gives Amazon instant credibility in the toy business, and using Amazon tells Toys R Us customers the company's disastrous shipping and availability problems of past years won't recur. It's a win-win-win situation, and in the Next Economy, all three wins will be necessary.

Or look at Martha Stewart and her relationship with K-Mart. The retailer needed a category success capable of driving traffic, and basics and housewares are major categories in the mass-merchandising business. Martha Stewart needed to get her brand more broadly supported and distributed in an environment she could control. Their joint success is probably strategically the single most important factor driving their growth.

SELLING SOLUTIONS

Comarketing allows you to focus on your customers by building a customized solution around their needs. Rather than worrying about the people you have on staff and how you're going to keep them busy, you enlist the talents you need to solve client problems, whether these talents are internal or external. This allows you to keep your costs reasonable, to employ top-notch talent for a fraction of the cost, and to present a uniquely customized solution to each client. It's a surefire recipe for turning customers into best customers.

Here's an example: Sun Microsystems is currently comarketing with its spin-off company, iForce, delivering full-service end-to-end offerings that are designed to meet a company's complete array of hardware, software, and database needs. IBM and several of the big consulting/accounting firms are doing similar things. Sun, IBM, and the others have figured out that the key to success is delighting your customer. It's almost impossible to do that within the confines of a huge infrastructure. If you have a huge infrastructure, you have a giant monster that must be fed—that is, it must be given work to do. But how can you delight your customer if the solution he or she wants isn't what you need to sell?

In time, solutions selling will migrate from the business-to-business (B2B) world into the business-to-customer (B2C) arena. Eventually, it will turn into a strategic approach rather than a tactical one—larger and permanent, not ad hoc. Temporary strategic partnerships will become closer and stronger relationships, creating a seamless feel for the customer. The result is a joint-custody customer.

Watch the evolution of customer management as broadcasters begin to master the ability to move slivers of their broad audiences from specific shows to Web sites to corporate brands. NBC and NBCi are beginning to actually use the new interactive technology the way it was envisioned. Broadcast will become the giant net that sweeps up all kinds of fish. Programs will organize these fish holistically into increasingly finite species (want segments). These will be enticed to visit specific NBCi pages or tune into a particular cable network, where an appropriate comarketing partner's message will be waiting.

The model: Increased relevancy through higher involvement levels, driving deeper relationships between brands and their best customers.

INTELLECTUAL PROPERTY AND COMARKETING

There's usually one quarterback in a comarketing deal, and usually this is the company with the initial customer relationship. Of course, protecting this relationship is important. Legal steps generally must be taken to prevent the partners you bring in from switching your customers to competitors in both the B2B and B2C worlds.

The quarterback company also should own and control the overall strategy of the customer solution they create. This is an example of how crucial intellectual capital will be in the next economy. The quarterback company is the one that figures out what's needed to solve the customer's problem and how to do it. The value of these insights is enormous and will need to be protected.

A lot of work will need to be done over the next several years to develop legal frameworks for the new intellectual capital game. Much old contract law is losing its relevance, and new rules must be established. For now, the key concepts are these:

- The role of the quarterback company will be to identify the customer opportunity to define a strategy, to find the best resources everywhere, and to establish clear legal agreements with all the partners.
- Compensation should be based mainly on successful outcomes, as measured by clear and consistent standards determined in advance.
- Each partner's revenue stream will be an annuity, representing not individual projects or products but a piece of the total flow that varies based on how successfully the solution is benefiting the customer.

Note that in this kind of relationship, money grows only out of the customer's success. This is crucial to maintain the clear customer-centric focus that every company will need in the Next Economy.

DEVELOPING A COMARKETING PROGRAM— A STEP-BY-STEP GUIDE

Remember that the objective of comarketing is to build relevancy with your best customers by developing a stronger bond than your brand could achieve on its own. Therefore, it stands to reason that your best customers are the people who can tell you which brands to consider partnering with and how to develop a program that will be meaningful to them. Here's the process I recommend.

Focus on Q_1 and Q_2

Start any comarketing effort with the top two quintiles of your customer base. The idea is to build relationships with other brands that are compatible with your best customers' familiar behavior. The more closely your comarketing program fits what your best customers are already doing, the more participation you'll enjoy.

Use Qualitative Research to Determine the Context of Consumption

Use focus groups, one-on-one interviews, and other qualitative research methods to uncover when, how, and why your brand is used. Most important, determine what other products or services are being used around the same time. You are seeking cross-consumption experiences during which other product or service categories interact with your best customers while they are using your brand.

Test Qualitative Conclusions with Quantitative Research

Based on your qualitative research, develop a hypothesis of compatible brands, categories, or events that appear to be closely linked to your best customers' brand experience. Then test this hypothesis through quantitative research with your Q_1 and Q_2 customers. Look for statistically valid correlations between your brand's consumption and the hypothesized compatibles.

Define and Pretest the Ideal Comarketing Program

Taking what you now know about how your best customers experience your brand, craft the ideal comarketing program for them, summarizing the benefits and risks for the cobrands, distributors, retailers, and most important, the customers. Once you have this program on paper, take it back to your customers and qualitatively test its acceptance.

Canvass Your Comarketing Prospects for Their Support

Here's where it gets tricky. The most important tool you have is the research into how category consumption correlates with your brand data. You may even have targeted a specific brand or two that is compatible with your brand's usage. Now you must decide how to use this knowledge.

In my experience, the brand leaders in any category tend to be the least flexible, the most bureaucratic, and the least entrepreneurial. Therefore, if you approach the number one brand in any category concerning a possible comarketing arrangement, be prepared to wait a long time for a response. Part of the challenge will be figuring out which entry point in the bureaucracy to approach with your proposal. Your best bet is to try the vice president level, where the information you've developed should find an interested and possibly motivated audience.

An alternative is to move down the brand rankings to the third or fourth player, where you are likely find much more flexible and entrepreneurial management. Your problem here will be to ensure that your distribution coverage is geographically compatible—that is, can the number three brand you want to work with reach all the customers you want?

Broaden the Club

Repeat the preceding steps as many times as needed to broaden your comarketing effort, based on the research you've already done. Always remember that you should ask your customers to make as little change in their consumption patterns as possible. The idea is to build a rewards program for your best customers—one that will give them what they want from you. In the long run, this will maximize your chances of getting what you want from them in return.

Formalize the Comarketing Arrangement

Have your lawyers create a document to be signed by all the comarketing partners, formalizing the program and the rights and responsibilities of each party and defining the intellectual property rights arrangements.

Monitor and Continuously Improve the Plan

Finally, set up regular meetings—monthly, bimonthly, or quarterly— among all the partners to review the results of the program and explore how to add value to the existing offerings.

WHO SPEAKS FOR THE CUSTOMER?

One major challenge for comarketing in the Next Economy arises from the current management structure of our companies. In the comarketing world, we'll need to understand how customer management can be shared between companies. It will become a priority as this marketing strategy gains momentum. And the implications for other aspects of corporate structure are significant

The marketing departments of most businesses are organized along pyramidal lines, which, as we've discussed, is terribly destructive. Because there's usually only one job available at the next higher level, it encourages an attrition-based warfare for promotions, leading people to do the right thing for their careers rather than for the customer or the brand.

In addition, marketing was and has been a staff job, with no bottom-line profit and loss (P&L) responsibility. The Next Economy will be marketing-centric. Marketing will be a line job, and people such as sales managers, customer service managers, and merchandisers will report to the marketing department. It's a necessary evolutionary step to support the essential new focus on customers and their wants.

If you're in any kind of comarketing situation, you're by definition sharing your customer relationships with other people and providing them with access to your customer base. To do this, you need to be able to open your customer books and share that information with other companies—something that is difficult for traditionally organized businesses to do. More important, you need to share with your comarketer a philosophy about how to nurture the customer relationship for the long term. The traditional business pyramid, focused on immediate results and short-term thinking, doesn't lend itself to longevity, brand-building, and relationship-building. Thus comarketing runs into difficulties when Old Economy companies try to practice it.

Here we can learn valuable lessons from the New Economy model. One of the by-products of the New Economy's fixation on speed to market was the evolution of outsourcing as a strategy. Initial public offering (IPO)–driven dotcoms didn't have the time to develop all the toys and whistles they needed to come out of the gate on time, so they sought "strategic alliances" with other companies that gave them the expertise they needed and the credibility with the financial community to move forward. How often did an alliance with Oracle, Microsoft, IBM, Nortel, or AOL drive a company's shares forward?

This type of strategic alliance competency must be grandfathered into the Next Economy. We see it developing through mergers and acquisitions. But that's an Old Economy financial model. You don't need to acquire shareholder equity in another company to become more relevant to your best customers. You do need access to their brand equity. This can be accomplished by restructuring the organization so that the comarketing merger has line authority over which brands in the marketplace best complement and extend the involvement level of your corporation's brand. However, this won't happen until marketers take line control over the customer relationship. And since this is the key to Next Economy success, marketers, by definition, will have to move into the chief executive officer (CEO) jobs to make this happen. They will.

In the 1960s, real estate drove corporate profits. The 1970s belonged to operations, the 1980s to finance, and the 1990s to information technologies. The 2000s belong to marketers. Restructuring the corporate organization chart to service best customers will become the first objective of many of them.

CONTROL OF THE CONTACT POINTS

As I have suggested, every brand has holistic contact points with its customers. These are the places where the brand and the customer touch each other in a physical and/or psychological manner. These places include

- Public relations
- Advertising
- Product packaging
- Displays
- The purchase
- Delivery

- Consumption (the product)
- Receptionist
- Call centers
- Follow-up service

Of these, marketing today controls only the first two and sometimes a portion of the product. Displays and distribution are sales' responsibility, not marketing. Yet every point of contact is a critical element in establishing a relationship with the brand. Display, purchase, and delivery have everything to do with the retailer/distributor and almost nothing to do with brand marketing. Is your product the first recommendation of the search engine? Is it an end-aisle display? Is it to the right of the front entrance of the store? Is it up during the key seasonal sales period? Is it delivered on time for the holidays? Does it come with a gift card? Is it wrapped appropriately? Does it cost what was promised? None of these relationship-building concepts are under the control of marketing.

Today, marketing controls only those customer contact points that deal with the promise. All the points related to the fulfillment of that promise—the purchase environment, product delivery, product design and quality, and so on—are not controlled by marketing. Nor are the points of contact related to resolution of problems related to the customer experience, such as receptionists, the call center, and follow-up service.

In the Next Economy, all customer contact points will be managed by the marketers. They will take control over the distribution contact points (the purchase environment and delivery), the customer consumption contact points (product design and quality), and the resolution contact points. Marketing will be responsible for the customer relationship and will need to manage all point of customer contact to enhance the brand equity.

As a result, fewer best-customer contracts will be broken, and the entire enterprise will be focused on enhancing its only real asset: a brand-loyal customer.

THE NEW CUSTOMER ADVOCACY

The structural issues are critical because we need to change who represents the customer at the boardroom table. What's required for the future is not product managers but *customer-care managers.* These will be professionals drawn from a series of disciplines—researchers, pricing experts, point-of-contact experts—organized in a new structure that represents the customer within the corporation. Their goals and objectives will be based on direct customer communications, not secondary or tertiary research. They'll constantly be talking to Q_1 and Q_2 customers to find out what they're doing with the brand, what they like and don't like about it, and what kinds of new products and services they wish they could get. And they'll cast a wide enough customer net to ensure that the results they gather are truly representative.

Is this a truly feasible scenario? Yes. Remember that the objective of consumer research used to be to find out what *all* customers were doing, thinking, and wanting. Quintile management changes this perspective. Now we recognize that the key is to understand how the quintiles interact with the brand. This is a much more focused objective.

In the Next Economy, the customer-care centers will be the front-line troops—the people who represent the eyes and ears of the company. Their ability to understand what delights customers will become a strategic competitive advantage.

Today, the marketing group has its own resource pool—researchers, ad agencies, pollsters, and others—which represents the company, not the customer. This arrangement won't work in the Next Economy. Instead, a dedicated Q_1 and Q_2 brand manager is needed. This brand manager should have all the marketing specialists reporting to him/her, and he/she will meet on a regular basis with his or her counterparts at other companies to compare notes and plans and constantly develop cobranding ideas and programs. The brand manager's job and that of his/her colleagues will be to focus their brand equity around those things which are important to their best customers.

Figure 9-1 illustrates how our corporate structures are changing and need to change in response to the demands of the Next Economy. Note that in the Next Economy model, all the points of contact between the customer and the brand fall under the direction of the marketing manager. This will permit corporations to develop consistently effective customer-care strategies for the first time.

Consider LVMH (Louis Vuitton Moet Hennessey) as an example of a company that will be operating in the Next Economy around their best-customer base—the high-end luxury buyer. This company is a

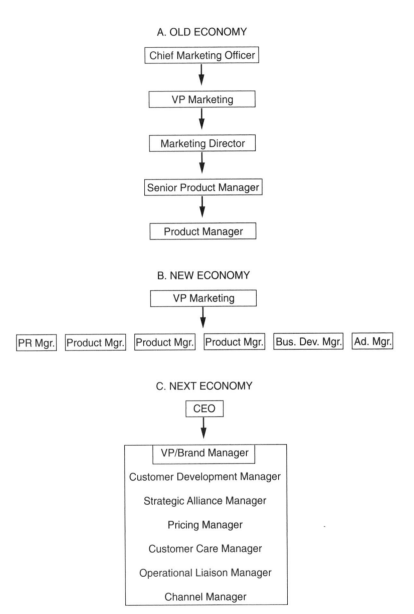

Figure 9-1 Corporate structures in the Old, New, and Next Economies.

precursor of the comarketing businesses of the future. For example, it could find itself in the premium travel business. In addition to fabulous cruises and weeks at little-known resorts, it could offer a high-level security program to protect people's houses and properties when they're traveling. It could get together with the people from Lexus, Mercedes, and Rolls-Royce to offer exclusive tours of the world's best automobile factories. It could throw open houses at great wineries and auction houses and antique dealers.

These ideas could represent comarketing at a powerful new level, driving the company's involvement level higher by making its brands move into gateways to other experiences and brands that its Q_1 and Q_2 customer base patronizes. This strategy takes relevancy to a new high. And it paves the way for the ultimate logical outgrowth of the comarketing strategy: the emergence of the new form of marketing I call *concierge marketing*.

The Advent of Concierge Marketing

We don't hunt to feed our families any more. McDonald's can provide us with all the red meat we want. If we tend gardens, we do so as a hobby, because Safeway can provide all the produce we'd ever want to eat. We don't have to collect water from the nearest stream because Evian takes care of it. We don't have to walk miles to work because Ford is there for us.

We outsource most of the necessities of life to corporations we trust to deliver the quality and consistency we expect. We do this in every area of our life where we lack the expertise, energy, time, or interest to manage what we want for ourselves. The companies to whom we contract these requirements are those which we believe have the necessary knowledge, efficiencies, and buying power we lack as individuals. And most of the time, this system works very well.

This is the whole idea behind *Concierge Marketing*.

In the Next Economy, we'll expand the number and kinds of outsourcing relationships we maintain. We'll outsource more and more of our consumption decision to specialists who will procure, package, deliver, and administer them for us. Concierge Marketing eventually will deal not just with our necessities of life but with a broad band of service that caters to our wants, saving us time, energy, and money in the process.

SOME PEOPLE WE TRUST

A *concierge* is someone who represents the buyer and makes sure that his wants are met in the best possible way. We buy products and services from many people, but we have a concierge relationship with only a very few.

We have a concierge relationship with our personal financial planner. We pay him not for transactions but for increasing the value of our portfolio, and we've agreed to let him represent us in making financial deals on our behalf. Of course, he will touch base with us if there's a significant decision, but because of his expertise and trustworthiness, we permit him to make minor transactions without discussing the details with us. He just reports back to us quarterly, and we review the results he has gotten for us. It's a relationship that works for both of us.

Another example of a concierge relationship: We own a house in Sarasota, Florida. To help us care for the house while we're in New York or elsewhere, we have a concierge relationship with a house sitter. He looks after our pool, exterminates every 3 months, checks the sprinkler, tends the lawn, and monitors the cleaning person. Right now, he brings all these service people to us, and we negotiate and pay for separate deals with each one. The next logical step, however, would be for him to handle it all without our personal involvement, for which he would get a basic fee and a percentage of the cost of the services provided. Perhaps we'll take this next business step some day.

Still another example: Our decorator, who is our concierge for home fashion. Before starting work on a project, she spends many hours with us discussing tastes, budget, etc. We write her a check for half the budget up front so that she can start buying all the furniture and hiring builders, painters, faux finishers, wood cabinet makers, rug people, art experts, "tchatchke" searchers, and so on. She will do the house from one end to the other, and it's possible we may choose to see only preliminary sketches and then the finished project when it's all put together.

Home builders are also a kind of concierge. They may not personally build anything. But they hire architects, computer programmers, roofers, plumbers, electricians, carpenters, and so on.

Why do we employ concierges in this way? We find that our quality of life—a major issue for aging baby boomers like us—is enhanced by having concierges. They free us to do only what we want to do. They have expertise and knowledge we lack. If my wife or I had a passion for decorating or investing, we might not use a concierge in those areas.

The Next Economy will move millions of customers into more and more relationships like this. I call the phenomenon *concierge marketing.*

WHY TODAY?

Concierge marketing is the converse of the old ways of buying and selling. The concierge will represent the buyer rather than the seller—a new approach to business.

In the past, marketing was concerned with the flow of goods and services toward customers. Now with all the changes we've talked about poised to affect the economy, it's inevitable that successful businesses will turn themselves into concierge marketers.

Concierge marketing isn't completely new. Commercial leasing is an area where concierge-like models have long existed. Many people in the leasing business represent the lessees rather than the owners.

There also have been some areas in the Old Economy where concierge relationships existed. The independent sales agent in a field such as insurance or stocks or financial planning supposedly would serve as an objective third party, with no vested interest in selling any specific product. However, these models were terribly abused. Spiffs started showing up—rewards paid by vendors—so that the independence and credibility of the agent's advice was undermined and his objectivity weakened. The moral is that you can *never* take money from both sides of a deal if you hope to earn the complete trust of either side. Other industries, including advertising, were undermined by the same conflict. Independent insurance agents, for example, naturally should have evolved into financial advisors—they should have taken the necessary educational courses and chosen to represent the customers alone. But they failed to do so and today are becoming obsolete.

Concierge marketing doesn't now exist except in a few fields such as travel agencies and interior decoration. And even these sometimes aren't true examples, since there are often built-in conflicts of interests: The travel agents often have a vested interest in hawking a few select tours and vacation packages. Good sales associates could and sometimes do represent the customer. But spiffs and incentives are rampant in many fields where the associates influence the sale. Thus they do not truly represent the best interests of the customer, although they may appear to do so.

The time has come for concierge marketing. As we've seen, generational issues are one reason. The concierge is ideally suited to an older, well-heeled market of people who want to focus their time and energy on activities they love.

Concierge marketing is the next logical evolutionary step beyond comarketing, especially for a generation of consumers that feels skeptical about dealing directly with suppliers. As we've seen, the seller-buyer relationship has been badly abused—no wonder the buyer no longer trusts us. And because she has no representation, the buyer is talking to her peer group for advice, guidance, and support. Advocacy groups are multiplying—chat has become big. There's a huge group of people who deal with sites that do nothing but give people an opportunity to vent their feelings about products and services. The trend illustrates how frustrated people are by the lack of representation for them as buyers.

The Net is replete with examples of how customers are taking control, using technology to fashion a solution. Lending Tree Financial Services brings vendors to bid for your financial services. Buy.com lets you comparison-shop for any stock keeping unit (SKU) on the Web. Amazon.com has reader reviews of the books for you to get an unbiased opinion. Privaseek and Safeweb allow you to surf the Web anonymously.

The whole peer-to-peer (P2P) technology is based on bypassing the infrastructure and controlling content and access. Napster was the beginning of the great battle for intellectual property, not the end. Sharing files is where the Net is going next.

The many sites for disgruntled employees and customers are another example of how buyers are gaining control over sellers. When American Airlines tried to reduce its fares to certain selected cities in order to stimulate traffic, the Web lit up with complaints from other cities. This all came about because Flyertalk.com brought together flyers in a number of cities to compare deals. The ability to regionalize the offering was taken away from American as word spread over the Net that the company allegedly was offering certain populations deals it was withholding from others. As the write-in campaign intensified, American reportedly had to reconsider the program.

This story demonstrates how the Internet, among other developments, is both enabling people to push harder for the satisfaction of their wants and providing them with tools to do so. More important, it reflects the shift of power from corporations to the individuals—especially customers.

Both the rate of explosion and the passion with which customers get involved in these advocacy sites are indications that customers want someone they trust to represent them. This stems from years of abuse of the customer contract. The extent of customer dissatisfaction and the intensity of their demands for better treatment mean that there is a deep unsatisfied desire to better these relationships. With few exceptions, customers don't have the time to interact with our bureaucracy, and they don't like the treatment they often get.

The Next Economy will change all this for a growing number of customer-brand relationships. Concierge marketing subjugates everything the company does to one goal: delighting the customer. It assumes the existence of a contract between the customer and the brand. The transaction is the signature to this contract and carries with it an implied commitment to the customer. In a concierge economy, people within the company will represent the customer's viewpoint through the whole process. Managing all points of customer contact will be key. The goal is to anticipate what the customer will want and provide it, thereby reinforcing the contract every time. We will adjust our company to her desires, not vice versa.

Notice how different this is from traditional ways of operating. In the Old Economy, there were individual functional silos inside the corporation. The extent to which the CEO could merge all the silos or at least get them to stop working at cross-purposes largely determined the success of the organization. We called it *Vision*. This wasn't easy to do; politics was always in the way.

The New Economy didn't do much to remedy this problem. The silos were still there, although they were different silos—IT, back end, marketing. Most important, the customer still played a small role in determining the shape of the organization and its priorities.

If the customer didn't buy the technology, it was because she didn't get it. In the next economy, she doesn't have to "get" anything. It'll be our responsibility as marketers to bring her what she wants. We're the ones who will have to get it.

As we've seen, every business has numerous points of contact with customers: advertising, promotional work, the website, research, product development, product quality improvements, distribution system, packaging. All of these will have to be managed from the customer's perspective—not ours, not our managers', not our shareholders'.

In the Next Economy, we will all sell services, not products. Relationships based on trust will drive the business. That trust will be based on the fact that, in effect, she is hiring us as a procurement manager for her, whether we are being paid by her or by our companies.

WHAT THE CONCIERGE WILL PROVIDE

A concierge relationship is an ongoing one. A once-a-year relationship isn't a real relationship—it's a transaction. To make it worthwhile, the concierge has to provide relevancy, expertise, and service through multiple contacts. Most of all, the concierge must be trusted.

Getting permission to act on the interests of your Q_1 and Q_2 customers will be the crucial challenge and the greatest reward of the Next Economy. Permission marketing will take on new meaning because of the extensive filters that concierges will need to understand exactly what their client wants from a category and which brands she has historically patronized.

Some of these brands will have enough equity to survive as "untouchables," nonnegotiable parameters of the concierge's task. Most who have no brand relationship will become susceptible to competitive offerings at the point of transaction. Of course, the very point of concierge marketing is that the buyer will now have as much expertise in the category as the seller. Therefore, relationships will have to be built using the Four R's to add value to the brand that would go beyond price as the sole discriminator. A professional buyer (that is, a concierge) understands that price is what something costs. Value is what it's worth.

My designated concierge in any area will have to know a lot about my preferences in order to represent me well. My travel agent will know that I'm an avid skier and love auto racing. She'll use software to find great deals on Grand Prix tickets or ski equipment, and she'll let me know that the opportunity exists to buy them from her.

Ultimately, I might have a half dozen concierges: an information/entertainment concierge, a food shopping concierge, a utilities concierge (dealing with TV, cable service, phone, fax, modem, and electricity, constantly changing my service providers as necessary, representing me, and paying my bills), and a travel concierge. Expertise filters will be the natural way this develops.

Conversely, one could have a single concierge representing the household for everything. However, I think the former arrangement is more likely, since we're paying for expertise that is generally unique to a particular field, not merely the transactional convenience. The point is to avoid the opportunity costs involved in having to learn all the complicated stuff one needs to know to consume complex products and services nowadays.

Finally, I might well designate my most trusted call center as my concierge for the category and perhaps even other corollary categories. Kraft Foods could well represent my grocery purchases. Firestone Customer Care could be my automotive concierge because of the superb job they did for me with tires and brakes. It's all a matter of deciding who has the expertise and who has earned my trust.

THE BEGINNINGS OF CONCIERGE MARKETING

Some corporations have already begun the battle for Concierge Marketing. American Express's platinum "Front of the Line" program is a concierge concept, focusing especially on travel. Early platinum users used to marvel at how the Front of the Line concept would allow them to buy hard-to-get tickets to great concerts, championship games, and other special events. The card provided upgrades in selected hotels as well as access to a world-class travel agency.

Some of the early gold cards broadened their packages to provide insurance, air miles, and customer help lines. Of course, many of these offerings are not promoted because it's in the best interest of the company not to have customers use the service. Talk about reverse strategy!

The Wyndham Suites hotel chain has a new program where you can request what you want in your room, and it will be prepared for you, allowing customers to design their own room with fax, particular kinds of toothbrushes, wall art, whatever they want. Thus the company is turning itself from a supplier of accommodations into a hospitality concierge.

Coldwell Banker now has a concierge service for its real estate customers that recommends movers, insurers, decorators, etc. The company is providing a service beyond just selling you the home. They are trying to become your concierge in the moving business—a service much broader and more relevant than real estate.

Progressive.com will get you three insurance policy quotes from different companies, acting as your agent, not its own.

The automobile makers are getting into concierge strategy. General Motors OnStar, Rescu from Ford, and Tel-Aid from Mercedes Benz are corporate-owned services available for buyers of top-end autos. The services provided vary. OnStar illustrates the idea. When you press a button, OnStar will unlock the car remotely; it also will send you roadside service immediately when your car breaks down, using a global positioning system (GPS) like those used for navigation by ship captains. OnStar is also planning to add many other services, including help with airline tickets and hotel or restaurant reservations. You pay a subscription fee with a special opening offer when you buy the car. The first year comes free with purchase of a Cadillac; then there is a variety of packages you can add on.

The window fashion business at Sears Canada is evolving to a concierge concept. When you're in the market for drapes or curtains, you come in and pick the window look you like. Sears will then bring together thousands of fabrics, materials, and brands that you can examine on the computer. You then order the drapes you like in the style and material your prefer. Sears doesn't have to inventory the fabric, and you get a much wider selection of styles than would otherwise be possible, all with the guidance of a trained home fashions expert.

Voyant Corporation is offering a new technology for eyeglass customers. The company takes your picture and then lets you see yourself in hundreds of different eyeglass frames. You can order the glasses you like over the Net or through participating ophthalmologists. The company will e-mail you an image of your face with new frames every quarter as new fashions become available. The company's Web site is a virtual encyclopedia of eye care, including a locater service for ophthalmologists. Clearly, Voyant doesn't just want to sell you glasses. It wants to become your eye-care concierge.

Reflect.com is a Web-based cosmetics company funded in part by Procter & Gamble. Reflect lets you get a customized makeup look from among 50,000 formulas available. You answer questions describing your hair color, your skin type, your favorite styles, and so on, and the company gives you a customized look. As of October 2000, this 2-year-old company had over 260,000 unique users per month.

And we've previously discussed how Purina Cat Chow is providing services to customers of its products through its Web site. At Purina.com, there are vets who specialize in cats, chat rooms about cats, all the information about cats you could want, etc. Thus Purina is providing a service, building trust, and—in effect—acting as your concierge for cat care.

Companies such as these are pioneering a new way of doing business. They are also insulating themselves from some of the upheavals that the advent of concierge marketing will cause for other, less farsighted companies. A concierge for cat care is needless as long as Purina.com is serving all those needs. Similarly, the Progressive.com Web site makes the independent insurance broker less necessary. *Intermediaries who currently represent sellers as go-betweens will have to switch sides—if they don't evolve into concierges, they'll be ruthlessly eliminated.* This includes most retailers.

HOW CONCIERGE MARKETING WILL SHAKE UP INDUSTRIES

Business structures that have served traditional marketing must be broken down to make them work in the Next Economy. In an age of economic withdrawal, it is inevitable that we will evolve in the direction of concierge marketing as we seek out best-customer relationships. Some companies will be so smart and will master the concierge approach so thoroughly that they'll be able to deal with customers directly. Only the best will be given this right. The rest of the world will find themselves dealing with professional buyers who will represent groups of individual customers. This will put businesses in a much tougher bargaining position.

To better understand the difference, consider how the high-end interior decorating business works today. The very best furniture stores have great decorators on staff who will help customers design their rooms, focusing not on the products they want to sell but on the customer's taste, budget, family size, and other specifications. Then they will do the necessary buying of furniture, fabrics, accessories, and so on, not only from their own inventory but from other suppliers' inventories as well. Stores that don't provide this kind of service gradually find themselves losing more and more of the high-end, profitable decorating and furnishings business to professional designers who represent their customers and can be counted on to be knowledgeable and tough buyers. This model gradually will spread to other businesses.

Where will the concierges of tomorrow come from? Many will come from the customer-care field—people who are running customer call centers today. They are on the front line of customer wants, and many of them understand that representing the customer is where the money is. Sociology and psychology majors will have new, more important roles to play in marketing to best customers. Researchers who have always understood the fragility of the brand–customer relationship are another source. The pool of talented, empathetic brand managers will be still another.

Not every field will be dominated by concierges. Remember, however, that in the future, the top third of the economy will drive 70 percent of purchases. The bottom half of the economy will be focused on needs rather than wants, and there's almost no money to be made in needs (except for the low-cost provider, e.g., Wal-Mart). The fashion business, for example, could be revolutionized by personal shoppers who would go to retailers or even manufacturers to purchase the brands and styles their customers favor. No longer working for the retailer, the shopping concierge would be empowered to negotiate price and evaluate alternatives on behalf of the customer. Suddenly, fashion retailing would take on a new meaning.

Similarly, the same average person might sign up with a car concierge. This concierge will give you an updated version of today's Onstar system. He or she will represent 5000 other car buyers and therefore will be able to get a great deal on your next car. He or she will bring it to your house for a test drive, handle routine service calls, provide a loaner car when yours is in the shop, take care of getting you a minivan or a little truck when it's time to drop your daughter off at college, help plan and arrange your fly-and-drive vacation to Europe, and so on.

As the car service example suggests, concierges will first become popular in areas where the average person doesn't have the expertise needed. This means that concierge marketing is going to shake up the structure of many industries. Companies that have long dominated their fields will find themselves losing market, losing customers, and (most scary of all) losing control over consumption. Companies that today play bit roles or don't even exist will rise to positions of power by virtue of their willingness and ability to represent their best customers. Companies in neighboring fields that understand the concierge concept will expand across today's industry borders. The result will be a dramatically reshaped business landscape 20 years from today.

I can't understand why retailers, who are closest to the customer, are so far refusing to invest in the marketing, research, and customer care they require to solidify this relationship. Buyers don't talk to vendors. Operations advice is not heeded by merchandising. Merchandising requests for displays are ignored by operations. And all the while, the entire organization responds in total chaos to the latest competitive discount flyer.

Retailers are intermediaries. If they don't become best-customer-driven and learn how to delight their Q_1 and Q_2 patrons, they will suffer terribly over the next decade. They have the most to lose in the transformation, but they are in the best position to evolve toward a concierge relationship with their customers. Sadly, most will do nothing.

CLOSE AS YOUR MORNING PAPER: THE CONCIERGE AS BRAND

A recurring connection is needed for a true concierge relationship, which is why retailers are so well poised for the concierge era. My local bank manager calls me once or twice a year, asking me to let her handle part of my investment portfolio. But my relationship with the bank is far from strong enough to support that level of trust. It so happens that I need to call the bank some 15 or 20 times a year about routine transactions—funds transfers and the like. When I do, I almost always get answered by voice-mail. Oh, the bank manager always calls me back—but it usually takes a day or two.

By contrast, my financial planner is on the phone with me religiously, at least once a month. (Unfortunately, not always with good news!) When I call her with a question, she picks up the phone herself. She'll get more of my investment business in the future—not my local bank.

Companies that are in continual contact with customers will have a better opportunity to become concierges. By contrast, companies with nonrecurring relationships and those which lack the frequency of action to be truly relevant to customers often will find themselves dealing with a concierge agent or forced to comarket with other brands that have the relevancy they lack.

Some of the best recurring relationships today exist in such industries as services, retail, the telcoms, financial services, e-tailing, and the daily media. In fact, newspapers and magazines are good examples of concierges today. A newspaper is a kind of concierge in the area of knowledge and information, acting as an information filter for their readers. A newspaper is also one of the best deals around—where else can you get access to so much intellectual property for pennies? A newspaper includes lots of knowledge condensed from much more information than we could ever hope to digest. Acting as our filter and with our tacit permission (as shown by the fact that we buy the newspaper daily), the editors simplify the mass of information down to the things they believe are most relevant to their readers. Editors are constantly aware of what their readers expect and want, and they scour the world looking for information that interests them. They also interface with readers daily, building equity. Newspapers provide the ability for customers to respond through many media—800 numbers, Web sites, letters to the editor, ombudsmen.

Thus newspapers provide a surprisingly good illustration of where the economy is going. Unfortunately for them, they haven't yet figured out how to broaden this relationship into other media or into the acquisition of other goods and services. In this segment of their business, they insist on representing the vendors (i.e., their advertisers) rather than their customers (i.e., the readers). Nor are they interested in providing different mixtures of information for each of their quintiles, which technology would certainly facilitate. They have a wonderful, multiple point of high-quality contact daily—too bad they are satisfied with only the tip of the iceberg.

Cable TV, which is narrowcasting rather than broadcasting, is also appropriate for the concierge economy. To be trustworthy and recognized as having expertise better than their customers, a concierge must be a brand, preferably one with strong personality. The Disney Channel on cable does this, whereas Disney-owned ABC does not. Instead, it takes a shotgun approach, much like the other broadcast networks. AOL could get there were it not for its current preoccupation with digesting the Time Warner acquisition, which I believe will distract its attention for most of the rest of this decade.

Today, the technology exists to turn broadcasting into narrowcasting. TiVo and the other new set-top systems let you act as your own entertainment concierge by programming in whatever you want the machine to record. Eventually, however, all this will be outsourced to an entertainment and information concierge who understands exactly what you like to see and will program your media experience for you. This is a clear illustration of the role of the concierge as an active filter for your consumption experience, one that every good home electronics retailer could be looking at.

EARNING PERMISSION

Concierge marketing will be the next big step in the evolution of permission marketing. There's a strong correlation between how much you know about customers and your potential effectiveness as a concierge. We will not get a true concierge economy until there is enough trust between the customers and the concierge that the latter can provide the level of service desired. This is where *permission marketing* comes in. This refers to the empowering of a company to represent a customer. This power comes from the information the company gets about the customer's buying habits, hopes, fears, concerns, and priorities. The more you know about a person, the better you can service her.

Thus, by definition, concierges won't succeed unless they know more about us than they do now. For example, my travel agent knows little about my hopes and fears; she only knows what seat on a plane I like. She has rudimentary knowledge of me—the airlines I like, the meals I like, and perhaps the time of day I like to fly. She doesn't know my hobbies, my interests, or those of my family. She doesn't know my work schedule. She doesn't know when my kids are available to travel or where they'd like to go. Thus two things stop her from becoming a concierge for me: the information she lacks and the fact that I'm not paying her enough to think about all these issues.

The first void could be alleviated with a long questionnaire and/or in-depth interview. This is permission marketing in action, because giving the information means giving her permission to represent me. The second void also could be alleviated if there was enough perceived value in my travel agent's possible services to me. Right now I can book all the same stuff she books for me just by going to the computer. So I don't perceive much potential value in her services as a travel agent. She'll have to come up with a greatly enhanced service plan to win my trust to that extent. But I like her, and I trust her. She rarely screws up the details. Her ability to manage my frequently changing travel schedule sometimes astonishes me. Thus I probably would entertain the notion of giving Melissa and her company a chance at handling more responsibility—if she asked for it.

THE CHALLENGING TRANSITION

As I've said, concierges will be housed either within your company or outside. If they are outside, it'll be much harder for you to sell and service customers effectively. Thus, becoming your best customers' concierge in your product category will be pretty important. It will require big mental and behavioral changes on the part of companies. Mickey Mouse customer relationship management (CRM) systems won't do the trick. Neither will technical support lines that make you wait 35 minutes for help. Many companies will offer services of this kind and claim to be customer concierges—but customers will recognize the difference and reject them.

Companies that actually want to be concierges will have to accept the idea that sometimes they must lead customers to other people's products. I am now working with several business-to-business (B2B) clients to get their consultants to accept this idea—that they have to be prepared to sell other people's products if that's best for the customers. However, to be customer-centric rather than technology-centric or product-centric is a hard leap for many companies to make.

IBM's consulting business is an example of an old-line company that has successfully begun this transition; IBM is satisfying customer desires using products and services from many vendors, not just IBM. Could another big tradition company like General Motors evolve to do this? Maybe not; the car makers are so bureaucratic and product-centric that this may be impossible. Maybe legal difficulties deter them. However, someone will take the plunge. Whoever gets there first will unquestionably expand their concierge mandate because the infrastructure will be in place for them to do so. Whoever owns the customer relationship will prosper.

THE IMPLICATIONS FOR BUSINESS

If they want to reconstruct their companies to be customer-centric, thereby opening up the possibility of operating as concierges, companies will have to make a number of far-ranging changes. Existing product-driven divisional silos will have to be redefined so that delighting the best customers becomes the overall goal around which all activities are focused. Consequently, companies will have to be led by marketing people—once marketing has been redefined along the lines I'm proposing in this book. This would represent a fundamental shift in business. As I've noted, in most companies, sales, finance, or operations people have risen to the top. Technology companies are often led by information technology (IT) people, and retail businesses are often led by merchants or operators. Thus, if marketing is to rise to the fore, we'll need some insightful and visionary brand managers.

Furthermore, our traditional measurements of business success must be changed if we are to represent customers appropriately. Instead of cost efficiency, response time (i.e., how quickly we can deliver the product to the customer) will become a more appropriate measurement. Similarly, IT should be judged on the basis of simplification rather than complication. The central goal must become making the black box of technology work more easily for customers.

Some may say that changes like these aren't really necessary. After all, aren't most companies today spending time thinking about their customers and their needs? Maybe so. But there are two problems with the way it's being done now.

First, those doing it have almost no power. Marketing is usually a staff job rather than a line job, which means that most marketers can't drive strategy they way it needs to be driven. Second, there's a huge disequilibrium in the customer-company relationship. The customer isn't spending anywhere near as much time thinking about the brand as we spend thinking about the customer—or as much as we'd like. This disequilibrium will only be changed when the degree of shared values and relevancy we can bring to the customer is greatly increased—and this requires shifting our companies' organization so as to be centered around the customer.

To succeed in this transition, companies will need to differentiate between consumer programs and customer programs. Consumers consume. They're the Old Economy target. But the word *customer* is derived from *custom*. A customer is an individual with distinguishable wants, concerns, and lifestyles. We must move our corporate priority to delighting the best of our customers at every point of contact.

A GOLDEN AGE FOR SMALL BUSINESS?

The age of concierge marketing will be ideally adapted to the flourishing of small to midsized business. Small businesses will be customers of concierges, who will serve businesses and meet their needs in every area from real estate to travel services to office management to information technology. Small business also will feed products to consumers through concierges. Their flexibility and ability to customize make small businesses especially suited to this style of business—far more so than the traditional, large, *Fortune 500* company.

The transfer of power to small companies is already in progress. For example, right now, during a period when many are announcing the death of e-commerce, small Web sites are doing great, especially those with annual sales under $1 million—bakeries, crafts, hobbies, small B2B operations, small retail operations. These sites are operating underneath the radar of the big players. They don't need huge volume to make e-business profitable; a small company can benefit from adding 14 customers a week to a 100-customer base. And because the interactivity of the Internet gives it amazing power to create customized products and services, the Net makes it possible to serve ever-smaller market niches with ever-more-precisely-tailored offerings, another huge opportunity for thousands of small companies.

Recognizing the growing importance of small businesses, the smartest of the big companies are now focusing on serving and supporting small business. Delivery giant UPS just bought Mail Boxes Etc. in order to gain entry to the small-business market. Office retailer Staples is opening a small-business service group in every store. American Express just launched a small-business concierge service. And Citibank is redesigning its credit card lines to be more responsive to the needs of small businesses.

Don't underestimate the power of small companies. Ninety percent of businesses employ fewer than 20 people [according to the National Federation of Independent Businesses (NFIB)]. Small businesses account for over 50 percent of private-sector output, 35 percent of gross domestic product (GDP), and two-thirds of all the new jobs created in the past 25 years. Their importance is likely to increase in the Next Economy. Will it be possible for larger companies to reconstruct themselves as needed to become concierges? This is a huge unknown. It will be a major survival issue for big companies in the near future.

My bet is on the little guy.

Epilogue: Your Company in the Next Economy

The duration of the Next Economy won't be measured in months, as was true of the New Economy. It will last about 20 years. Therefore, it is important to understand how to strategically prepare your organization for the transition into this whole new way of doing business.

THREE ERAS, THREE ECONOMIES

The matrix shown in Figure E-1 summarizes the differences among the Old Economy, the New Economy, and the Next Economy. Let's go through the nine elements in the matrix and discuss what each one means for your business.

Business Priority

What motivated or preoccupied the leaders of the business? In the Old Economy, it was product—you made things. This was the business you were in, starting with the industrial revolution up till the mid-1990s. In the New Economy, it was information. Technology was used primarily to get information faster to individuals. However, information has no inherent value until you do something with it. In the Next Economy, it

Figure E-1 Old, New, and Next Economies

	Old Economy	New Economy	Next Economy
Business priority	Product	Information	Knowledge
Success measure	Market share	Revenue	Profits
Investment rationale	Scale	Efficiency	Effectiveness
Leading function	Operations	Infomation technology	Marketing
Managerial mindset	Econocentric	Web-centric	Customer-centric
Corporate structure	Pyramidal	Flat	Team-oriented
Financial base	Debt	Equity	Debt/equity
Sales target	Consumers	Vendors	Customers

will be knowledge. We'll take products and services from the Old Economy and marry them to information technology from the new economy and use the combination to cater to customers. We'll be in the knowledge business, meaning knowledge of the priorities, desires, and concerns of customers, as well as knowledge of what's available to satisfy them in the marketplace.

Success Measure

How was success measured? In the Old Economy, it was share of market. This is why economies of scale were critical and why it was considered crucial to grow bigger and bigger. Being the low-cost producer was the ultimate goal, since the idea was that rationalizing production through efficiency would make profits almost automatic. Thus companies spent time and money capturing market share and then defending it—spending on slotting, shelf space, sales incentives, and so on.

In the New Economy, it was revenue—first "eyeballs," then revenue. The revenue chase planted all the seeds for technology, justified investments, and drove the business models and the "space" you operated in. In the Next Economy, we'll be driven by profitability, which will come from perceived added value that best customers will not question because they'll see it, know it, appreciate it, and be willing to pay for it.

Investment Rationale

When people were asked to invest, what was the rationale? In the Old Economy, it was scale—meaning economic size and dominance of market. If you were a blue chipper, a top player in a particular marketplace, or had scale internationally or through vertical integration, this was thought to lead ultimately to profitability. And if you had scalability, people wanted to invest in you.

In the New Economy, the priority was efficiency. The idea was to get rid of intermediaries and clean out all the excess from the system, streamlining operations and going direct to customers wherever possible. People paid for efficiency.

In the Next Economy, it will all be about effectiveness—adding an intermediary back in who will represent buyers and can find the right service, the right product, the right information. It's not a matter of quantity but quality—not just doing things right but doing the right thing.

Leading Function

What part of the organization dominated the business? In the Old Economy, it was operations and finance. In the New Economy, it was information technology. In the Next Economy, it will be marketing.

Managerial Mindset

What did the leaders of corporations focus on? In the Old Economy, it was econometrics. Companies were concerned mainly with economic measurements such as scalability, where you stood in the oligopoly, overhead costs, and so on. Business was dominated by an econocentric model, which reflected what was valued by the Securities and Exchange Commission (SEC) and the stock market. The New Economy was Web-centric, built around the belief that technology would automatically capture customers. As a result, the Web became the California gold rush of the 1990s. But as we've seen, there was a lot of fool's gold out there. In the Next Economy, we'll be customer-centric. The management priority will be to organize the company around adding value to the customer relationship.

Corporate Structure

How are companies organized? In the Old Economy, the typical structure was pyramidal, encouraging silo management. It created an organizational culture that was very political, draining productivity from the corporation and often subverting the brand. Worst of all, in a pyramidal structure, for every winner there are 10 losers, which means lots of turnover, little brand continuity, and broken customer contracts.

In the New Economy, businesses were supposed to be flat, nonhierarchical, and collaborative. Unfortunately, this made no sense in the real world. I've sat in many meetings at companies supposedly run through collaborative processes. They usually valued each voiced opinion equally. The result was the ultimate management-by-committee concept, driven largely by inexperienced executives seeking refuge in watered-down, safe, or irrelevant decisions—stuff that worked in the boardrooms but failed in the living rooms of North America. Thus the New Economy produced a lot of camels—horses designed by committees, as the old saying has it.

In the Next Economy, concierge teams will be the dominant organizational form. Groups of customers will be assigned to people in organizations who form teams organized in support of a concierge, who might be in charge of working with the customers in a particular state, customers of a certain want segment, or customers of a certain quintile value or frequency of involvement with the corporation. This internal customer representative will lead a team that will provide answers, which might include a pricing expert, a production expert, a Web master to customize the Web page, etc.—all of whom will be part of the team. There will be individual responsibility within the context of functional expert teams.

Financial Base

How is business growth financed? The Old Economy was based on debt. This meant that before you got your money, the financial institutions pored over the numbers, the history, and the industry data to ensure that your company was healthy. They were looking for a company that would be in debt continually and therefore making interest payments for years to come. This generated very profitable working relationships between companies and their debt providers.

In the New Economy, growth was financed by equity. The expected payback period was often weeks or months, not years as in the Old Economy. Thus the business objective of the venture capitalist was to go public fast and improve on product technology on the fly. In their rush to get in and cash out, the venture capital community supported technologies that weren't ready for customers. But they didn't care. For the most part, they had no intention of holding onto the stock any longer than necessary. Thus the relationship between the customer and technology seemed unimportant.

In the Next Economy, it will be a new combination of debt and equity. Speed to market will no longer be the key. Instead, it'll be building long-term customer relationships.

The equity portion could well be customer-driven. One aspect of the ultimate concierge economy is that customers often will own a part of the businesses, a concept that brings the concierge idea to a perfect full circle. After all, why would you buy someone else's brand when you own part of the company? In boardrooms I'm now visiting, this conversation is already happening. Take a car manufacturer as an example. In the future, instead of offering a $1600 rebate on your next Ford, they'll give you $1600 worth of Ford Motor Company stock. Already, 54 percent of households own stock directly or indirectly. In many cases, brokers and financial advisors are making financial decisions for these families as concierges. Extending this idea to include stock ownership as part of the concierge model for consumer spending will require working out many financial and legal details, but it is a natural step.

Sales Target

How did the sales force make its money? (This determines in reality what the company does.) In the Old Economy, salespeople got paid on how well they managed distribution. The sales forces got paid either for selling directly to customers or for pushing product through the retail channels. In the vast majority of these situations, the salesperson's payment consisted of a base salary plus a commission. The belief was that if you own the shelf space, you own the sales. In fact, Point of Purchase Association International (POPAI) has been saying for years that if you own the last foot of the distribution chain, you own the whole thing. The problem with this idea can be seen in the current impotence of marketing. For years, a growing share of the marketing money has been put into insatiable distribution demands for funds.

In the New Economy, the leading sales objective was signing up vendors. If you were a portal, you tried to make money on advertising while practically giving away products or services. The customer had very little to do with this—hence its limited success. As we've come to realize, "eyeballs" don't spend money—people do. And you can't continually sell advertising on the basis of hits when real revenue only kicks in with a purchase.

In the Next Economy, the customer will pay. The concierge economy is based on a subscription model—the daily newspaper business expanded to the world. Yes, there will be some advertising, but the brand value delivered to the individual customer will be great enough that the best customers will willingly pay a high enough price to drive profitability.

NOWHERE TO HIDE

Historically, in every decade since the 1960s, the economic impact of the baby boomers has come as a surprise to most businesspeople. In each decade, it took us about 5 years to adjust to the new realities. The adjustments were painful organizationally, but most companies were able to remain profitable because, for the most part, the adjustments occurred in a climate of strong overall growth.

The shift to the Next Economy will be as wrenching a change as any we've experienced in the past. But with a difference: This time there will be no 10 percent economic growth to cushion the adjustments business must make. If this shift occurs on your watch, you're in for a difficult ride. And there will be no sectors of the economy immune to the challenges. All of us, whether we like it or not, are about to be participants in what historians probably will call the greatest economic restructuring since the industrial revolution.

The journey to the Next Economy is about to begin. Will your company be ready?

The Next Steps

The impact of the Next Economy on the current business model means that marketing will have to lead the charge in building corporate profits for the coming 15 to 20 years. The challenges will be enormous; the economic conditions we'll face will be unprecedented. And the ideas in this book are only a start in the search for new solutions. Therefore, as we move forward, the opportunity for us all to learn from each other's successes and failures is perhaps the most valuable asset we can leverage.

If you wish to share your comments or discuss your experiences in coping with the evolution of the Next Economy, you can e-mail me at thenexteconomy@ettenberg.com. Depending on the level of interest and dialogue, I'm hoping we can begin a quarterly "virtual newsletter" chronicling marketing successes and failures while providing a venue for exchanging new ideas on how to cope with the restructuring of corporate America as it begins to focus on the need for best-customer marketing. I hope to hear from you soon.

Elliott Ettenberg

Notes

INTRODUCTION

Page xi. Nearly half of Americans now own stock. James M. Pethokoukis, "Mania Mania: Stock Market Was Never More Valuable, Nor More Volatile," *US News & World Report*, April 3, 2000.

CHAPTER 1: FROM OLD ECONOMY TO NEW ECONOMY TO NEXT ECONOMY

Pages 6–7. Statistics concerning e-commerce spending, 1999–2000, and projections to 2005. *The Forrester Brief—The Forrester Report*, April 18, 2000.

Page 21. Over half of the would-be online shoppers—63 percent to be exact—canceled orders... Jupiter Media Metrix survey, June 11, 2001.

Page 22.... The rate of abandonment of e-tail shopping carts is very high... Matthew Schwartz, "The Care and Keeping of Online Customers," *Computer World*, January 8, 2001.

CHAPTER 2: MARKETING IMPOTENCE

Page 28. One American turns 50 every 6 seconds. Martha Ramsey, Director of Publications, American Association of Retired Persons, AARP News Release, September 25, 2000.

Page 29.... Two-thirds of all gross domestic product is driven by consumers... National Income and Product Accounts Tables, Bureau of Economic Analysis, U.S. Department of Commerce, Washington, July 27, 2001.

Page 29. The savings rate, which has been shrinking for decades, is now negative. "United States: The Kiss of Life?" *The Economist*, April 21, 2001.

Page 34. Consultant Fred Reichheld of Bain and Company... Fred Reichheld, *The Loyalty Effect*. Harvard Business School Press, Boston, Mass., 1996.

Page 36. North American businesses now spend about $170 billion per year on advertising. American Association of Advertising Agencies.

Page 41. One or both of these dubious techniques. John A. Byrne, *Chainsaw: The Notorious Career of Al Dunlap*. Harper Business, New York, 1999.

Page 44. According to POPAI, the in-store decision rate for packaged goods and grocery items. *1995 Consumer Buying Habits*, Point-Of-Purchase Advertising Institute in conjunction with Meyers Research Center.

CHAPTER 3: THE RISE OF CUSTOMER POWER

Page 54. A study by Richard K. Green. "Demographics Don't Support New-Store Boom,"*Chain Store Age*, May 1, 1998.

CHAPTER 4: THE FAILURE OF THE FOUR P'S

Page 68. Today, there's a Radio Shack within 5 minutes of 94 percent of the U.S. population. Company Fact Sheet, RadioShack, Inc.

Page 73. Consequently, long-distance companies and ISPs are incurring enormous customer acquisition costs. The Strategis Group, Inc.

CHAPTER 5: THE BIRTH OF THE NEXT ECONOMY

Page 83. According to Cardatta.com, the top four branded credit cards. Robert McKinley, CEO, CardWeb.com, July, 2001.

Page 84. The Health Insurance Association of America says that over 40 percent of all people. *Consumer Information/Guide to Long Term Health Care*, Health Insurance Association of America, December, 1999.

CHAPTER 6: WANT SEGMENTATION

Page 94. Unilever recently expanded its distribution efforts into the poorer regions of India. Rekha Balu, "Strategic Innovation: Hindustan Lever," *Fast Company*, 47.

CHAPTER 7: QUINTILE MARKETING

Page 125. According to a September 2000 InterActive Consumers Study from Cyber Dialogue, the top 20 percent of online shoppers. "The 90/20 Rule of E-Commerce: Nearly 90% of Online Sales Accounted for by 20% of Consumers," Cyber Dialogue Press Release, September 22, 2000.

CHAPTER 10: THE ADVENT OF CONCIERGE MARKETING

Page 195. As of October, 2000, this 2-year-old company had over 260,000 unique users per month. Alison Stein Wellner, "Beauty in Distress," *American Demographics*, January 2001.

Page 202. Ninety percent of businesses employ fewer than 20 people. William J. Dennis, Jr., *A Small Business Primer*, NFIB Education Foundation, August 1993. *Small Business Answer Card*, Small Business Administration, Washington, 1998.

Index

About the Author

ELLIOTT ETTENBERG is the Chairman and Chief Executive Officer of Customer Strategies Worldwide Inc., New York, and the founder of Ettenberg & Company Ltd., a Strategic Think Tank operating from Glen Sutton Quebec. These companies advise large consumer-based corporations on how to maximize shareholder value by developing a sustainable competitive advantage with their Best Customers. Elliott pioneered and developed the strategy of building rapid brand loyalty by exponentially increasing the impact of the marketing budget on its most critical asset, the top quintile of the customer base.

Before founding CSW and E&C, Elliott was Chairman and Chief Executive Officer of Bozell Retail Worldwide, New York, where he managed the development of retail and other high transactional client businesses on a global basis. Prior to Bozell, Elliott was the Chairman and Chief Executive Officer of Prism Communications Ltd., a leading advertising and marketing communications company operating from Toronto and Atlanta. He sold the company to Bozell Worldwide in 1996.

Elliott is widely published on the topic of consumer marketing. His comments and opinions have appeared in numerous business publications including *Fortune, Business Week, The Economist, The Wall Street Journal,* and *The New York Times.* He has keynoted regularly in North America, Europe, and Asia on upcoming consumer trends and has appeared on CNNfn and CNBC as a consumer expert. He has a Masters of Business Administration from Concordia University in Montreal.

You reach Elliott at: elliott@ettenberg.com

or

ettenberg@customerstrategies.com